It's Another Ace Book from CGP

This book is for 14-16 year olds.

First we stick in all the <u>really important stuff</u> you need to do well in the GCSE Double Science Chemistry Foundation Paper.

Then we have a really good stab at making it funny — so you'll <u>actually use it</u>.

Simple as that.

CGP are just the best

The central aim of Coordination Group Publications is to produce top quality books that are carefully written, immaculately presented and marvellously funny — whilst always making sure they exactly cover the National Curriculum for each subject.

And then we supply them to as many people as we possibly can, as <u>cheaply</u> as we possibly can.

Buy our books — they're ace

Data Page

The Periodic Table

Group O

Periods
1

You should be pretty familiar with the 31 elements shown shaded.

You don't really need to know much about the others.

Mass number →

Atomic number →

Group I	Group II												Group III	Group IV	Group V	Group VI	Group VII	

Period 1:
- 1 H Hydrogen 1
- 4 He Helium 2

Period 2:
- 7 Li Lithium 3
- 9 Be Beryllium 4
- 11 B Boron 5
- 12 C Carbon 6
- 14 N Nitrogen 7
- 16 O Oxygen 8
- 19 F Fluorine 9
- 20 Ne Neon 10

Period 3:
- 23 Na Sodium 11
- 24 Mg Magnesium 12
- 27 Al Aluminium 13
- 28 Si Silicon 14
- 31 P Phosphorus 15
- 32 S Sulphur 16
- 35.5 Cl Chlorine 17
- 40 Ar Argon 18

Period 4:
- 39 K Potassium 19
- 40 Ca Calcium 20
- 45 Sc Scandium 21
- 48 Ti Titanium 22
- 51 V Vanadium 23
- 52 Cr Chromium 24
- 55 Mn Manganese 25
- 56 Fe Iron 26
- 59 Co Cobalt 27
- 59 Ni Nickel 28
- 64 Cu Copper 29
- 65 Zn Zinc 30
- 70 Ga Gallium 31
- 73 Ge Germanium 32
- 75 As Arsenic 33
- 79 Se Selenium 34
- 80 Br Bromine 35
- 84 Kr Krypton 36

Period 5:
- 85.5 Rb Rubidium 37
- 88 Sr Strontium 38
- 89 Y Yttrium 39
- 91 Zr Zirconium 40
- 93 Nb Niobium 41
- 96 Mo Molybdenum 42
- 99 Tc Technetium 43
- 101 Ru Ruthenium 44
- 103 Rh Rhodium 45
- 106 Pd Palladium 46
- 108 Ag Silver 47
- 112 Cd Cadmium 48
- 115 In Indium 49
- 119 Sn Tin 50
- 122 Sb Antimony 51
- 128 Te Tellurium 52
- 127 I Iodine 53
- 131 Xe Xenon 54

Period 6:
- 133 Cs Caesium 55
- 137 Ba Barium 56
- 139 La Lanthanum 57
- 179 Hf Hafnium 72
- 181 Ta Tantalum 73
- 184 W Tungsten 74
- 186 Re Rhenium 75
- 190 Os Osmium 76
- 192 Ir Iridium 77
- 195 Pt Platinum 78
- 197 Au Gold 79
- 201 Hg Mercury 80
- 204 Tl Thallium 81
- 207 Pb Lead 82
- 209 Bi Bismuth 83
- 210 Po Polonium 84
- 210 At Astatine 85
- 222 Rn Radon 86

Period 7:
- 223 Fr Francium 87
- 226 Ra Radium 88
- 227 Ac Actinium 89

The Most Basic Stuff of all — you must learn your elements

1) _Chemistry_ is all about _knowing the differences_ between the various elements and compounds.
2) And one thing's for sure — if you don't know the really _basic_ information about all the elements that you come across, then you've no chance of sorting anything else out.
3) This page contains _really basic stuff_ on elements.
4) The _position_ of each element in the _Periodic Table_ determines the whole of its _chemical behaviour_.
5) _At the very least_ you must know where all the 31 shaded ones are.
6) You must also learn the _Reactivity Series for Metals_ shown below — _all the common ions_ are useful too.
7) Practise all three regularly by covering up parts of the tables and trying to remember what goes where.

The Reactivity Series of Metals

1) **Potassium**
2) **Sodium**
3) **Calcium**
4) **Magnesium**
5) **Aluminium**
   (Carbon)
6) **Zinc**
7) **Iron**
8) **Lead**
   (Hydrogen)
9) **Copper**
10) **Silver**
11) **Gold**
12) **Platinum**

Common Ions You Really Should Know

1^+ ions	2^+ ions	3^+ ions	$4^+/4^-$	3^-	2^- ions	1^- ions
Li^+ (lithium)	Mg^{2+} (magnesium)	Al^{3+} (aluminium)	Very rare	Fairly rare	O^{2-} (oxide)	F^- (fluoride)
Na^+ (sodium)	Ca^{2+} (calcium)	Fe^{3+} (iron(III))			S^{2-} (sulphide)	Cl^- (chloride)
K^+ (potassium)	Ba^{2+} (barium)					Br^- (bromide)
Cu^+ (copper(I))	Cu^{2+} (copper(II))					I^- (iodide)
Ag^+ (silver)	Fe^{2+} (iron(II))					NO_3^- (nitrate)
H^+ (hydrogen)	Zn^{2+} (zinc)	_Note that copper and iron can both form two different ions._			SO_4^{2-} (sulphate)	OH^- (hydroxide)
NH_4^+ (ammonium)	Pb^{2+} (lead)				CO_3^{2-} (carbonate)	
These lose **one** electron to form 1^+ ions.	These lose **two** electrons to form 2^+ ions	These lose **three** electrons to form 3^+ ions	These have a devil of a job gaining or losing three or four electrons.		These gain **two** electrons to form 2^- ions	These gain **one** electron to form 1^- ions

Contents

Published by Coordination Group Publications Ltd.
Typesetting and layout by The Science Coordination Group

Coordinated by Paddy Gannon BSc MA

ISBN 1-84146-519-4

Groovy website: www.cgpbooks.co.uk

Printed by Elanders Hindson, Newcastle upon Tyne.

In the Laboratory

Q1 The items of apparatus below are drawn in three dimensions. _Draw_ a _two dimensional_ picture of each item in the space given, then _write_ its name and state what it is used for.

a)

Name: Test tube

Used For: Doing simple experiments or chemical reactions with.

b)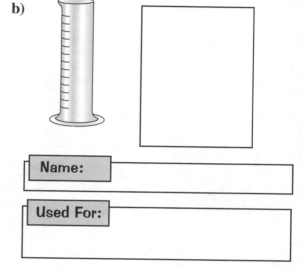

Name:

Used For:

c)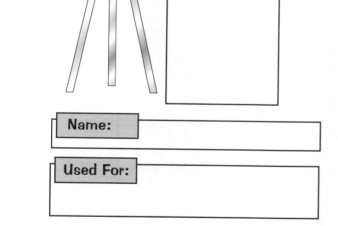

Name:

Used For:

d)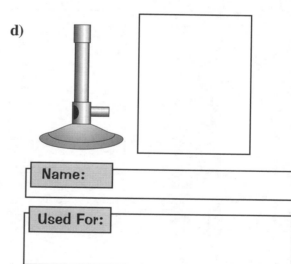

Name:

Used For:

e)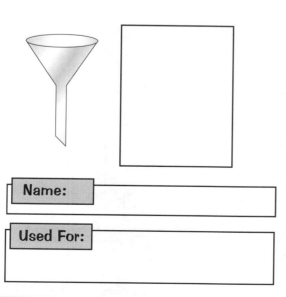

Name:

Used For:

f)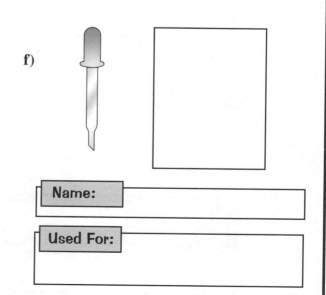

Name:

Used For:

In the Laboratory

Q1 *Draw* the apparatus next to each drawing, then *name it* and *give its use* in the laboratory.

a)

Name :

Used For :

b)

Name :

Used For :

c)

Name :

Used For :

d)

Name :

Used For :

e)

Name :

Used For :

f)

Name :

Used For :

Questions on Units

Q1 *Link up* the correct unit and unit symbol with each measurement below.

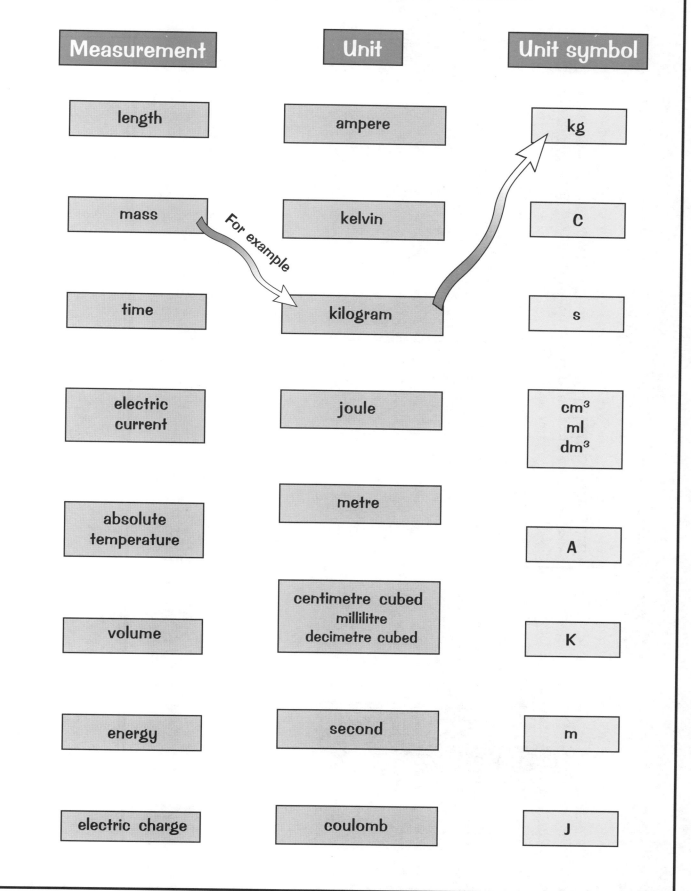

Measurement	Unit	Unit symbol
length	ampere	kg
mass	kelvin	C
time	kilogram	s
electric current	joule	cm³ ml dm³
absolute temperature	metre	A
volume	centimetre cubed millilitre decimetre cubed	K
energy	second	m
electric charge	coulomb	J

For example

Questions on Reading Scales

Q1 *Read the scale in each picture carefully and then <u>write</u> the measurement, including the* correct units, in the spaces provided:

a)

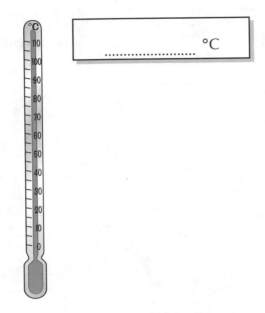

.... °C

b)

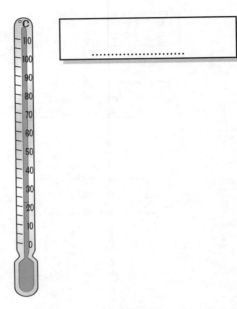

....

c)

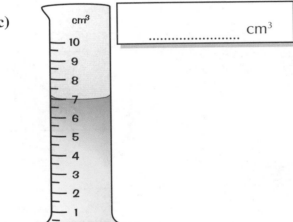

.... cm³

d)

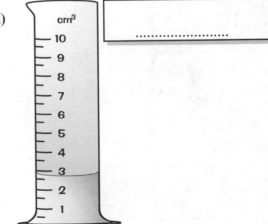

....

e)

.... g

f)

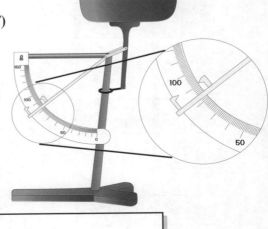

....

Questions on Reading Scales

g)

.... mm

h)

....

i) What is the depth of the froth?

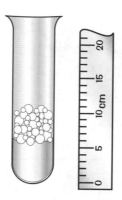

....

j)

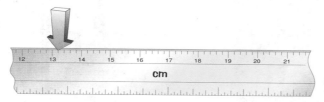

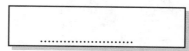

.... cm

k) What is the time shown by the stop-clock?

.... h .... min .... s

Questions on Hazards

Q1 *Draw arrows to link up* the hazchem symbols with the description.
Then give an example of each:

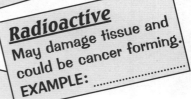

Highly Flammable
Catches fire easily.
EXAMPLE: ....

Toxic
Can cause death either by swallowing, breathing in, or absorption through the skin. EXAMPLE: ....

Irritant
Not corrosive, but can cause reddening or blistering of the skin.
EXAMPLE:
....

Harmful
Similar to toxic but not quite as dangerous.
EXAMPLE: ....

Corrosive
Attacks and destroys living tissues, including eyes and skin.
EXAMPLE: ....

Radioactive
May damage tissue and could be cancer forming.
EXAMPLE: ....

Oxidising
Provides oxygen which allows other materials to burn more fiercely.
EXAMPLE: ....

Explosive
Can explode in the presence of a naked flame.
EXAMPLE. ....

Q2 *List* six *safety hazards* you can see in this laboratory.

a) ....

b) ....

c) ....

d) ....

e) ....

f) ....

SECTION ONE — IN THE LABORATORY

Questions on Hazards

Q3 Why do we have a system of hazchem symbols, and why are they pictures, not just words?

....

....

Q4 _Describe_ how you would handle a "corrosive chemical".

....

....

Q5 Look at the following information found on the side of a chemical tanker.

a) Why is a hazchem symbol included in the information? ....

....

b) Why might the emergency services require _more_ information than just the hazchem

symbol? ....

c) Why is a _phone number_ included? ....

....

Q6 _A tanker overturns in a crowded shopping area leaking a chemical onto the road. The hazchem label tells the emergency services that the chemical is corrosive, they will require full body protection, but can wash the chemical down a drain._ Write a brief summary of the important steps a fire officer handling this accident should take.

....

....

....

....

Questions on Prefixes

Prefixes are sometimes added before a unit to show how BIG or how SMALL the number is.

Example:

1 kilogram = 1000g   "kilo-" means 1000 times or 10^3 times the number.

So 1kg = 1000g   and   1kN = 1000N

Use the tables below to help you find the answers to the questions that follow:

Prefix number	Which means times	Prefix	Symbol
10^9	1,000,000,000	giga	G
10^6	1,000,000	mega	M
10^3	1,000	kilo	k
10^2	100	hecto	h
10	10	deca	da

Prefix number	Which means times	Prefix	Symbol
10^{-1}	$1/10$	deci	d
10^{-2}	$1/100$	centi	c
10^{-3}	$1/1,000$	milli	m
10^{-6}	$1/1,000,000$	micro	μ
10^{-9}	$1/1,000,000,000$	nano	n

Q1 Circle the following symbols which you think are correct, and cross out those which you think are wrong.

a) kg   **b)** KN   **c)** kn   **d)** Am   **e)** MW   **f)** KV   **g)** mm

h) KA   **i)** DN   **j)** mA   **k)** kJ   **l)** ms   **m)** kN   **n)** dm³

Q2 *Complete* the following:

a) 100 g = ... kg

b) 1 kJ = ... J

c) 0.2 kg = ... g

d) 0.1 kJ = ... J

e) 100 mA = ... A

f) s = ... ms

g) 1000 N = ... kN

h) 100 N = ... kN

Questions on Prefixes

Q3 Complete the following conversions:

a) How many grams are there in 2 kilograms? ....

b) $1m^3$ = ... cm^3?

c) 100kJ = ... J?

d) Is one decimetre cubed larger or smaller than $10\ cm^3$? ....

e) How many amps are there in 1 milliamp? ....

f) How many amps are there in 10 milliamps? ....

g) Which is longer — 100 milliseconds or 1 second? ....

Q4 To get an idea of the scale of things in this world, _match up_ the following quantities with the correct numbers. The _correct unit_ for each quantity is already written in for you.

Quantity	Number	Unit
a) How many seconds are there in a year?	230	V
b) What is mains voltage?	3	V
c) How many volts would a torch run off?	2,400	w
d) How many volts would a personal stereo run off?	31,536,000	s
e) What is the wattage of a kitchen kettle?	about 110	no units
f) How many elements are there?	3	V
g) Radius of the Earth	4.6×10^{16}	m
h) Distance to the nearest star other than the Sun	6.37×10^{6}	m
i) Speed of light	3.00×10^{8}	m/s
j) Speed of sound in air	27	m/s
k) Fastest sprinter in the world	55	kg
l) Motorway speed limit	12	m/s
m) Fastest land animal in the world	31	m/s
n) Mass of an average woman	330	m/s

Know Your Apparatus

Complete the following crossword concerning laboratory apparatus.

Across

4) Measures temperature *(11)*

6) Funny-shaped vessel — not comical *(7,5)*

7) Burner *(6)*

9) Placed under jars when collecting a gas — (where bees live) *(7)*

10) Triangle of metal and pot *(8)*

11) A little baby test tube *(8)*

15) Sounds French — begins with a "b" *(7)*

16) Three-legged device, used to heat things on *(6)*

17) You keep test tubes in them *(4)*

18) Container — its name kinda rings *(7)*

19) Store gases in them *(3,3)*

20) Should always be worn when using chemicals *(7)*

Down

1) Timing device *(4,5)*

2) A large test tube *(7,4)*

3) Used to measure a volume of liquid *(9)*

5) Dish used to remove a water from salt *(11)*

8) Rod — made of glass, used for...... *(8)*

10) Little porcelain bowl *(8)*

12) Used to react things in *(8)*

13) Cheap pipette — but don't let go of it *(7)*

14) Always used when heating substances *(4,3)*

15) Used to mix substances in, not used to measure a volume *(6)*

18) Rubber _____ *(4)*

Questions on Charts and Graphs

Q1 *The diagrams below show the various ways that experimental results can be represented.*

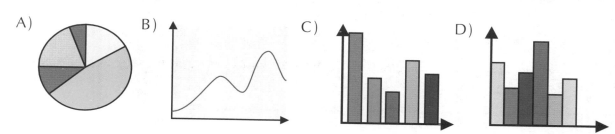

A)   B)   C)   D)

a) Write the *names* of the graphs in the white boxes below and then write the correct letter
(A, B, C or D) next to the name to *match up* with the examples above.

(i) [ ]
— shows the amount of each quantity in proportion to the size of each rectangle.

(ii) [ ]
— shows data like a bar chart but with no gaps between bars and a continuous horizontal axis.

(iii) [ ]
— shows how one variable changes smoothly with another changing variable.

(iv) [ ]
— represents each category as a proportion using area. Each category is a sector of the chart.

Q2 Which type of graph would you use to represent the data shown in each table below.

Element	% element in the sea
oxygen	85.7
hydrogen	10.8
chlorine	1.9
sodium	1.1
magnesium	0.14
other	0.36

Time (s)	Vol. hydrogen (cm^3)
0	0.0
1	2.2
2	3.6
3	4.4
4	5.2
5	5.5
6	5.5

a) .... **b)** ....

Q3 State *which graph* you would use for the following.

a) To show how long *different lengths* of magnesium ribbon take to react with acid.

....

b) To show the *% composition* of elements in the human body.

....

c) To show for *how long* three different sized lumps of limestone will react with acid.

....

CLASSIFYING MATERIALS

The Three States of Matter

Q1   Matter can be found in three different states.   Name the _three states_ of matter.

....

Q2   Name the _theory_ that explains the major differences between these states of matter.

....

Q3   In each of the boxes below, _complete the diagram_ to show the arrangements of the particles in the three states of matter _(each has been started for you)_.

Name: ....   Name: ....   Name: ....

Q4   The following phrases describe the properties of each state of matter and the arrangement of particles in each one. List each phrase in the appropriate column of the table at the top of the next page.

weak attractive forces between particles   particles in fixed position

random arrangement of particles   no forces of attraction

no definite shape   definite volume

particles in constant random motion

regular lattice arrangement   definite volume   no definite volume

strong attractive forces   no strength   can't be compressed   particles free to move

little strength   random arrangement of particles   particles in constant rapid and random motion

low density   particles free to move

often strong

little particle movement   can be compressed

very dense   quite dense   no definite shape

can't be compressed

The Three States of Matter

Solid	Liquid	Gas
E.g. very dense		

Q5 Matter is strongest in which state? ....

Q6 Which state will have the least number of particles in a certain volume? ....

....

Q7 For a given substance, in which state will its particles have the most kinetic energy?

Explain why. ....

....

Q8 a) Which _state_ will water be in at: **i)** -10°C **ii)** 10°C **iii)** 110°C _(at atmospheric pressure)?_

i) .... **ii)** .... **iii)** ....

b) What is the _common name_ for each state of water? ....

Q9 a) Why is it _difficult_ to compress liquids? ....

....

b) _Give an example_ of something that might use this property. ....

Q10 _Explain_ how a gas exerts pressure on a surface. ....

....

....

Questions on Changing State

Q1 Give two *everyday* examples of each of the three states of matter. ....

....

....

Q2 *Complete* the following diagram by naming each change of state — A, B, C, and D.

A

B

| Solid | | Liquid | | Gas |

D

C

Name: A = ...   Name: B = ...

Name: D = ...   Name: C = ...

Q3 *When heat energy is supplied to a substance, the particles absorb the energy and start to move about more.*

   a) What is the name of the type of energy the particles have when moving about like this?

....

   b) What happens to the distance between particles as the heat energy is increased?

....

   c) What must break for a liquid to change into a gas?

....

Q4 *Look at the graph opposite. This shows how the temperature of wax changes as it is cooled.*

   Explain why the graph has two flat sections.

....

....

....

....

Temperature

Cooling

gas

condensing

Boiling Point

liquid

Melting Point

freezing

solid **Time**

Q5 *Describe* what happens to the particles in wax when it freezes. ....

....

....

Questions on Changing State

Q6   *Use the table below to answer the questions that follow it.*

Substance	Melting Point (°C)	Boiling Point (°C)
Zinc	420	907
Oxygen	-238	-183
Bromine	-7	59
Mercury	-39	357

a) What temperature is *room temperature?* ....

b) Which element melts at the *lower temperature* — oxygen or mercury? ....

c) Name an element that is a *solid* at room temperature. ....

d) Name an element that is a *liquid* at room temperature. ....

e) Name an element that is a *gas* at room temperature. ....

f) Name an element that is a *liquid* at a temperature of *60°C*. ....

g) Name a substance that is a *solid* at both room temperature and *200°C*. ....

h) Name a substance that is a *liquid* at room temperature, but a *gas* at *100°C*. ....

i) *Explain* what happens to the particles in a *solid* as it is heated and changes to a *liquid*.

....

....

....

....

j) *Explain* what *evaporation* is. ....

....

....

....

....

SECTION TWO — CLASSIFYING MATERIALS

16

Questions on Diffusion

Q1 _Explain_ the term _diffusion_. ....

....

Q2 _Complete_ these sentences using these words:

fast	heavier	light	slower	kinetic

At a certain temperature the particles in a gas have a particular amount of

movement energy (_____ energy).

If the particles are _____ , then the speed at which they move will be

high and so diffusion will be _____ . If the particles are _____ ,

then the speed of the particles is small and so diffusion will be _____ .

Q3 _The diagram below shows pieces of cotton wool soaked in hydrochloric acid and ammonia._

Hydrochloric acid

Ring of white
ammonium
chloride
powder

Ammonia (solution)

White smoke appears where the two gases meet.

Hydrogen chloride + Ammonia → Ammonium chloride

a) Name the _process_ where the ammonia travels through the air to meet the hydrogen

chloride. ....

b) The _relative formula mass_ of ammonia (NH_3) is 17 and the _relative formula mass_ of hydrogen

chloride (HCl) is 36.5. Which substance is the _lighter_ of the two? ....

c) From the diagram, which substance has diffused the _furthest (quickest)?_ ....

d) What is the link between the _speed_ at which particles move and their _mass?_

The lighter the particles in the gas, the ....

....

SECTION TWO — CLASSIFYING MATERIALS

17

Questions on Atoms and Molecules

Q1 *Match* each picture to the correct statement by writing the letter(s) in the space provided.

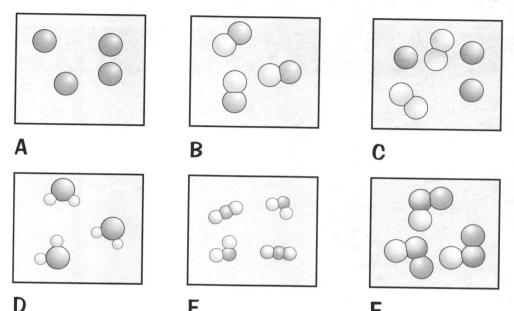

A **B** **C** **D** **E** **F**

a) A *pure* element — ....

b) A *pure* compound — ....

c) A *mixture* of elements — ....

d) A *mixture* of compounds — ....

e) An example of molecules made from just *two elements* — ....

f) An example of molecules made from *three elements* — ....

g) Which example could be *water (H₂O)?* — ....

h) Which example could be *carbon monoxide (CO)?* — ....

2) In the molecular model of silicon dioxide *(sand)* shown opposite, what are *A, B* and *C?*

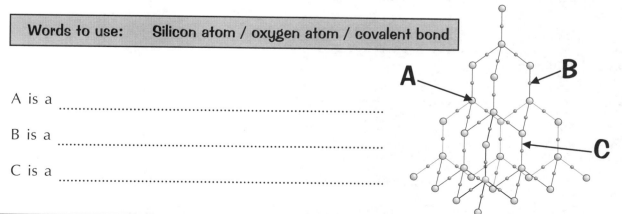

Words to use: Silicon atom / oxygen atom / covalent bond

A is a ....

B is a ....

C is a ....

SECTION TWO — CLASSIFYING MATERIALS

Elements, Mixtures and Compounds

Q1 _Complete the table_ by putting a tick in the correct column. The first one has been done for you.

Substance	Element	Mixture	Compound
Copper	✓		
Air			
Distilled water			
Brine			
Sodium			
Cupro-nickel			
Sodium chloride			
Copper sulphate			
Sulphur			
Oxygen			
Sea water			
Bronze			
Petrol			
Blue ink			
Steel			
Steam			
Milk			

Q2 Give a definition of an element. ....
....

Q3 Give a definition of a compound. ....
....
....

Q4 Give a definition of a mixture. ....
....
....

Q5 What is an alloy? ....

Q6 Why is an alloy not classed as a compound? ....
....
....

SECTION TWO — CLASSIFYING MATERIALS

Elements, Mixtures and Compounds

Q7 In the boxes below _draw out circles_ to represent atoms of elements and molecules of compounds. _(Note: use different colour or size circles to represent different elements.)_

A pure element	**Two molecules of two different compounds**
A pure compound	**A mixture of two elements**
A mixture of three compounds	**Three molecules of one compound, made of three different atoms**
Three atoms of one element	**A mixture of one element and one compound**

Questions on Solubility

Q1 *Below is a table of different substances and their solubilities at different temperatures. The solubility is the amount of the substance that will dissolve in a given amount of water, at a certain temperature.*

Plot a graph of solubility against temperature for each substance. Draw each curve using a different colour.

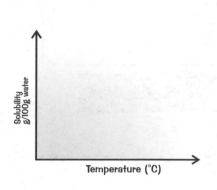

SUBSTANCE	SOLUBILITY (g/100g of water)				
	10°C	30°C	50°C	70°C	90°C
Ammonium Chloride	33	41	50	60	71
Copper Sulphate	17	24	33	47	67
Lead Nitrate	44	60	78	97	117
Potassium Chlorate	5	10	18	30	46
Potassium Chloride	31	37	43	48	53
Potassium Nitrate	21	45	83	135	203
Sodium Nitrate	80	96	114	135	161

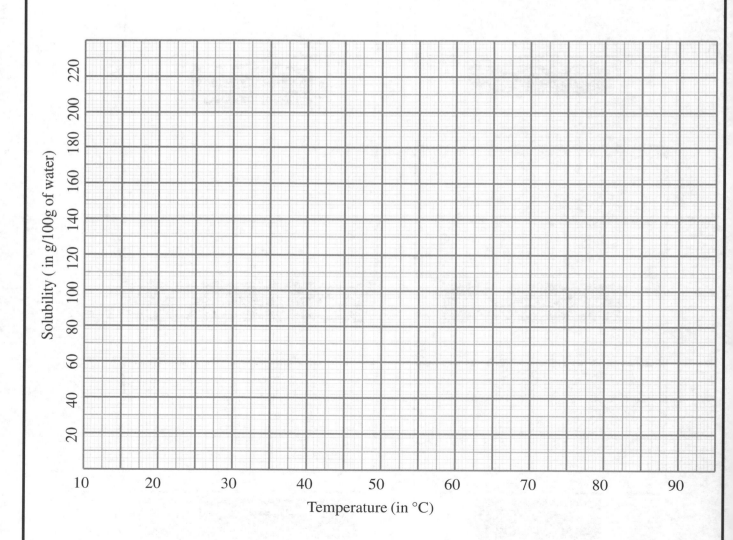

Questions on Solubility

Q2 Answer the following questions using the graphs you have just drawn.

a) Which is the most *soluble* substance at **i)** 10ºC **ii)** 30ºC **iii)** 50ºC **iv)** 70ºC **v)** 90ºC?

i) .... **ii)** .... **iii)** ....

iv) .... **v)** ....

b) What is the *solubility* of potassium nitrate (in g/100g water) at:

i) 15ºC **ii)** 60ºC **iii)** 75ºC? *(Big hint...... look at your graph for this question.)*

i) .... **ii)** .... **iii)** ....

c) Which substance's solubility *increases the most* between 10°C and 90°C? How do you

know? ....

....

d) If you cooled a 100cm³ of saturated potassium nitrate solution which contained 100g of

water, from 60ºC to 15ºC, *how much* salt (in grams) would fall out of the solution?

Show your working out.

....

....

.... Answer = ... g

Q3 *4g of a solid make a saturated solution with 50g of water.*

What is its *solubility* in g/100g of water? ....

Q4 *Describe* how you could approximately measure the solubility of sugar in water at 50ºC in

the lab. *(What apparatus will you need, what will you measure and how will you measure it?)*

....

....

....

....

....

Questions on Types of Materials

Q1 Give an _everyday example_ of the following materials, then _complete_ the rest of the table by using the following words: high, medium, low, good, poor.

Type of material	Common Examples	Tensile strength (how difficult it is to break apart)	Compressive strength (how difficult it is to crush)	Flexibility (how easy it is to bend)	Electrical conductivity (how easily it lets electricity through)	Thermal conductivity (how easily it lets heat through)	Porosity (how well it soaks up water)	Cost of manufacture
Metals								Expensive
Ceramics								Cheap
Glass								Expensive
Plastics								Fairly expensive
Fibres	Nylon Clothes							Natural: cheap, synthetics: fairly expensive

Q2 Work out the following types of materials or substances by _rearranging_ the letters.

a) SIDAC		g) BRISEF	
b) LISKALA		h) SCLASTIP	
c) LOLYAS		i) DOOW	
d) SREFTILISER		j) MARCCISE	
e) SPOAS		k) LAGESSS	
f) SLATS		l) TALEMS	

Questions on Atoms

Q1 *Answer these questions on atoms.*

A _____

a) What is an *atom?* ....

.... **C** _____

b) *How many* different types of particles make up an atom?

....

c) Give the *names* of the particles that make up an atom.

i) ....

ii) ....

iii) ....

B _____

d) Label the diagram above using the words: *nucleus, electron, and electron shell.*

Q2 *Complete* the table below using: *1, in the nucleus, 1/1836, outside the nucleus, 0, 1.*

Particle	Mass	Charge	Where it is found
Proton	1		
Electron		-1	
Neutron			In the nucleus

Q3 *Where* is most of the mass of an atom concentrated? ....

Q4 *Is this statement true or false: "Most of an atom is empty space"?* ....

Give a reason: ....

....

Q5 *Below is shown the symbol for Lithium.*

a) What do the letters *A* and *Z* in the diagram stand for? ....

....

A ⇘ 7
Li
Z ⇗ 3

b) *How many* protons are there in an atom of lithium? ....

c) *How many* electrons are there in an atom of lithium? ....

d) *How many* neutrons are there in an atom of lithium? ....

e) Which *number (A or Z)* determines the element that an atom is? ....

Questions on Electron Arrangement

Q1 The structure of an atom is often compared to the solar system. *Explain* why this is.

....

....

Q2 What keeps the electrons *attracted* to the nucleus? ....

Q3 *Complete* the table to show the maximum number of electrons in each shell.

Electron shell	Maximum number of electrons in the shell
1st	
2nd	
3rd	

Q4 *Complete* the table below showing the properties of the first 20 elements.
(You will need to use the Periodic Table near the front of the book).

Element	Symbol	Atomic Number	Mass Number	Number of Protons	Number of Electrons	Number of Neutrons	Electronic Configuration	Group Number
Hydrogen	H	1	1	1	1	0	1	—
Helium	He	2	4	2	2	2	2	0
Lithium	Li						2, 1	1
Beryllium							2, 2	2
	B			5			2, 3	3
Carbon							2, 4	
Nitrogen		7					2, 5	
Oxygen					8		2, 6	
Fluorine							2, 7	
Neon							2, 8	
	Na	11	23				2, 8, 1	1
Magnesium							2, 8, 2	
		13	27	13	13	14	2, 8, 3	3
Silicon							2, 8, 4	
Phosphorus							2, 8, 5	
	S						2, 8, 6	
Chlorine							2, 8, 7	
Argon							2, 8, 8	
							2, 8, 8, 1	1
Calcium						20	2, 8, 8, 2	2

Q5 Look at the table. What is the link between *group number* and *number of outer electrons?*

....

Q6 What is the link between the *Noble gases* (Group 0) and *full outer shells* (energy levels)?

....

Q7 The *number of electrons* in the outer shell governs which *properties* of the element?

....

Questions on Electron Arrangement

Q8 Draw the _full electronic arrangement_ for the elements in the following dot and cross diagrams, using crosses to represent electrons. Then write out the electronic configurations in the spaces provided. _(The first three have been done for you)._

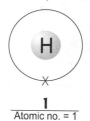

1
Atomic no. = 1

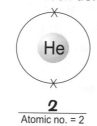

2
Atomic no. = 2

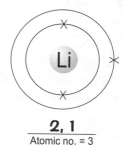

2, 1
Atomic no. = 3

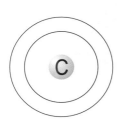

Atomic no. = 6

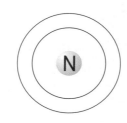

Atomic no. = 7

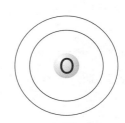

Atomic no. = 8

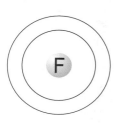

Atomic no. = 9

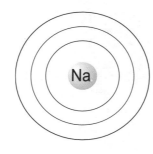

Atomic no. = 11

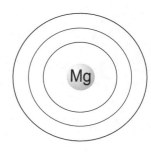

Atomic no. = 12

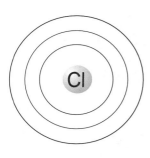

Atomic no. = 17

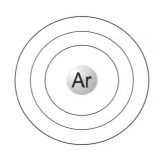

Atomic no. = 18

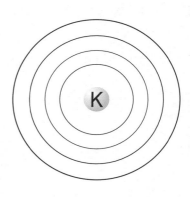

Atomic no. = 19

SECTION TWO — CLASSIFYING MATERIALS

Questions on Covalent Bonding

Atoms join up to make <u>molecules</u>. They do this by forming chemical <u>bonds</u>. A chemical bond always involves <u>electrons</u>. A covalent bond is one where atoms <u>share</u> one or more pairs of electrons. This means that both the atoms can effectively have a <u>full shell</u>. A full shell is a more stable arrangement of electrons. The noble gases have a full shell which means they are <u>inert</u> or <u>very stable</u> as they don't need to react. In summary, atoms undergo chemical reactions to attain a <u>full shell</u>, which makes them <u>more stable</u> — and that's why atoms react to make compounds...

Q1 What is a *molecule?*

Q2 What is a chemical *bond?*

Q3 What is a *covalent bond?*

Q4 *Draw* two crosses on the circles below to represent the electrons in a single covalent bond.

Q5 Why do atoms *share* electrons?

Q6 Which group of the periodic table do the atoms "try to be like"?

Q7 *Draw out* the electron configuration of neon ($^{20}_{10}$Ne) — only show the outer electron shell.

Questions on Covalent Bonding

Q8 Which of the following is the electronic configuration of chlorine ($^{35.5}_{17}Cl$)?

A) 2,8,6   B) 2,8,7   C) 2,7   D) 2,8,8,7   Answer = ...

Q9 *How many more* electrons does chlorine need in order to have a "noble gas" configuration *(i.e. — a full outer shell)?*

....

Q10 Using the diagram below, *draw out* the electron arrangement in a chlorine molecule. *(Draw outer shells only).*

Q11 Tick which in the following list are true regarding the *general properties* of covalently bonded molecules.

	True	False
a) Low boiling point.		
b) Soluble in water.		
c) Conductor when melted.		
d) Non-conductor when solid.		
e) Weak forces attract molecules to each other.		
f) Crystalline.		

Q12 If any of the properties listed in question 11 are false, then *correct them* in the space below. (E.g. if they've not got a low boiling point they must have a high one).

....

....

....

....

Questions on Ions

Na^+	H_2O	C	NO_3^-

Q1   Which of the above substances are examples are *ions?* ....

Q2   Give *one* example of an ion made from a single atom. ....

....

Q3   Give *one* example of an ion made from several atoms. ....

....

Q4   *Complete* this paragraph using the words provided.

-ve   protons   negatively charged   neutral   positively charged

Atoms are electrically _____ because they have equal numbers of

_____ (+ve) and electrons (____). If electrons are taken away from a metal

atom or hydrogen, then they become _____ _____ because it

has less electrons than protons. If electrons are added to a non-metal atom, it becomes

_____ _____ because it then has more electrons than protons.

Q5   Write the correct example next to each of the following descriptions.

SO_4^{2-}	Mg^{2+}	Kr	MgO	CO_2

a) An example of a gas consisting of *single atoms*. ....

b) An example of a compound made from *ions*. ....

c) An example of a compound made from *molecules*. ....

d) An example of a simple *ion*. ....

e) An example of a *molecular ion* (compound ion). ....

Questions on Ions

Q6 *The following electron transfer diagram shows what happens when a lithium atom reacts with a chlorine atom.*

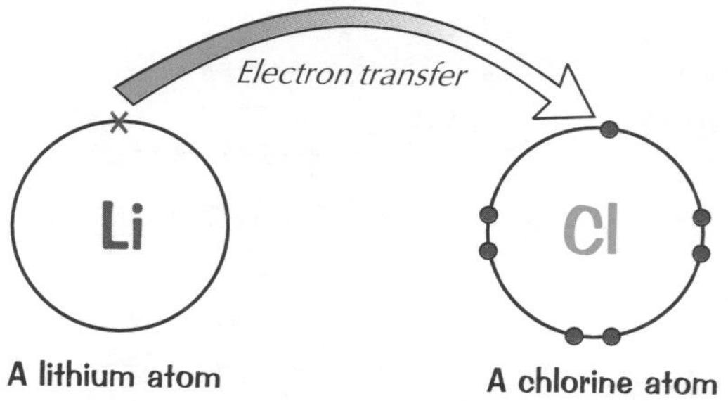

Name the compound formed.

....

Electron transfer

Li

Cl

A lithium atom

A chlorine atom

Q7 *Draw* an electron transfer diagram to show what happens when a sodium atom reacts with a chlorine atom.

Q8 Why do sodium ions have a 1⁺ charge? ....

....

Q9 Why do chloride ions have a 1⁻ charge? ....

....

Q10 If Group 1 ions have a 1⁺ charge on them, what charge would you find on a Group 2 ion?

....

Q11 What is a cation and what is an anion? ....

....

Q12 The diagram opposite shows a crystal of sodium chloride. Why is the sodium chloride crystal not charged — i.e. electrically neutral?

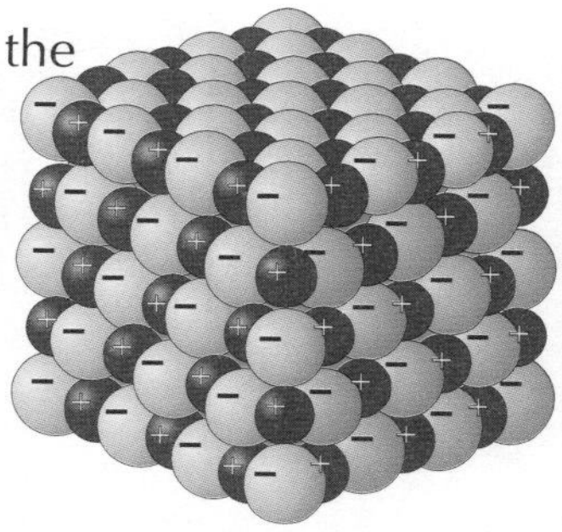

....

....

....

Questions on Symbols and Formulae

Q1 *Write out* the symbols for the following.

| iron | | lead | | zinc | | tin | | copper | |

Q2 *Complete* the following.

> When CHLORINE reacts with a metal element to make an
>
> ionic compound it forms a CHLOR _____ .

> When OXYGEN reacts with a metal element to make an
>
> ionic compound it forms an OX _____ .

> When SULPHUR reacts with a metal element to make an
>
> ionic compound it forms a SULPH _____ .

Q3 If a compound has *"—ate"* in its name, (like copper sulph*ate*), what *element* will be present?

....

Q4 *Complete* the missing information in this table:

Name	Formula	Ratio of each element present in the substance
Zinc oxide	ZnO	1 zinc 1 oxygen
Magnesium oxide		1 magnesium 1 oxygen
Sodium chloride	NaCl	
Hydrogen chloride	HCl	
Sulphur dioxide		1 sulphur 2 oxygens
	CO_2	1 carbon 2 oxygens
Sodium hydroxide		1 sodium 1 oxygen 1 hydrogen
Potassium hydroxide	KOH	
Copper sulphate		1 copper 1 sulphur 4 oxygens
		1 calcium 1 carbon 3 oxygens
Potassium nitrate	KNO_3	
Sulphuric acid	H_2SO_4	
Iron oxide		2 Iron 3 oxygens
	$MgCl_2$	1 magnesium 2 chlorines
	H_2	2 hydrogens
Chlorine		2 Chlorines

SECTION TWO — CLASSIFYING MATERIALS

Questions on Symbols and Formulae

Q5 Some toothpastes contain sodium monofluorophosphate. Name the four _elements_ you think are present in this compound.

....

....

Q6 Using the information in the table fill in the correct formulae for the compound.

Compound	Positive ion	Negative ion	Formula
copper oxide	Cu^{2+}	O^{2-}	CuO
sodium chloride	Na^+	Cl^-	
zinc sulphate	Zn^{2+}	SO_4^{2-}	
potassium iodide	K^+	I^-	
potassium hydroxide	K^+	OH^-	
calcium carbonate	Ca^{2+}	CO_3^{2-}	
lithium bromide	Li^+	Br^-	
potassium chloride	K^+	Cl^-	
copper sulphate	Cu^{2+}	SO_4^{2-}	
magnesium sulphate	Mg^{2+}	SO_4^{2-}	
potassium nitrate	K^+	NO_3^-	
lead sulphate	Pb^{2+}	SO_4^{2-}	
potassium bromide	K^+	Br^-	
lithium chloride	Li^+	Cl^-	
silver nitrate	Ag^+	NO_3^-	
sodium nitrate	Na^+	NO_3^-	

SECTION TWO — CLASSIFYING MATERIALS

Questions on Structures

Q1 *Below is a diagram that classifies substances according to their structures.*

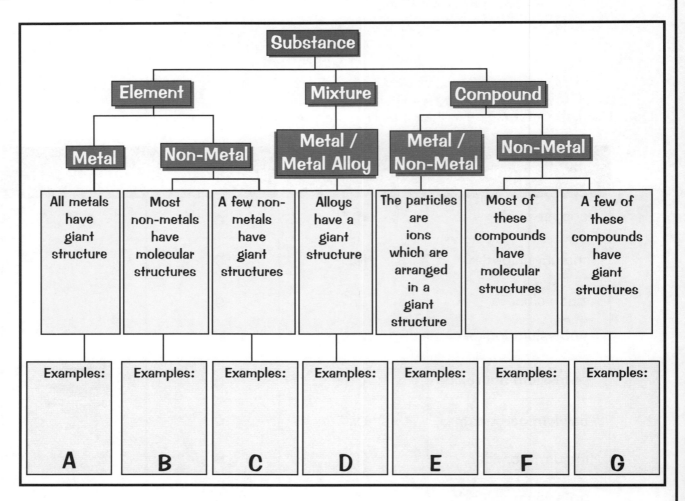

a) Write an example of each substance in the example box at the bottom of the above diagram.

b) Match the following examples with the correct boxes A → G. The first is done for you.

Cupro-nickel   **D**

Carbon   ☐

Potassium iodide   ☐

Magnesium   ☐

Sulphur dioxide   ☐

Phosphorous trichloride   ☐

Zinc   ☐

Sodium chloride   ☐

Questions on Structures

c) Match the following examples with the boxes A → G in the diagram on the previous page.

Hydrochloric acid ☐	Carbon dioxide ☐
Oxygen ☐	Potassium chloride ☐
Iodine ☐	Silicon dioxide ☐
Calcium ☐	Copper ☐
Silicon ☐	Copper sulphate ☐
Phosphorous ☐	Bronze ☐

Q2 _Complete_ the table to summarise the properties of different types of structure. Use the words, High / Low to state whether the materials have a high or low melting point, and use the words, Yes / No for whether they conduct or not.

High / Low   **Yes / No**

Bonding	Structure	Melting point	Boiling point	Do they conduct?		
				Solid	Liquid	Aqueous solution
Ionic	Giant					
Covalent	Giant					
Covalent	Molecular					
Metallic	Giant					Not applicable

Q3 A newly discovered substance X has the following properties:

- it has a melting point of 801°C
- it will conduct electricity when dissolved in water
- it is made up of crystals

Describe what you predict the bonding and structure to be like for substance X.

....

....

....

Questions on Metals and their Structure

Q1   *Metals have "giant structures of atoms".*
Which statement best describes the *giant structure* of a metal?

A) A regular arrangement of metal ions.
B) A regular arrangement of atoms sharing electrons
C) An irregular crystal.

Answer = ...

Q2   The first column in the table below lists some general properties of metals. Complete the table by writing a good example of each property, the reason why the metal has that property, and then state a metal that is an exception and does not have that property.

Metal Property	Good Example	Reason	Exception (if any)
Strong			
Good Conductor of Heat			
Good Conductor of electricity			
Can be rolled into sheets (malleable)			
Can be drawn into wires (ductile)			

Q3   What is an *alloy?* ....

....

Q4   Why do we *use* metal alloys? ....

....

Q5   Look at the diagram below. *Explain* why the alloy is *stronger* than the pure metal.

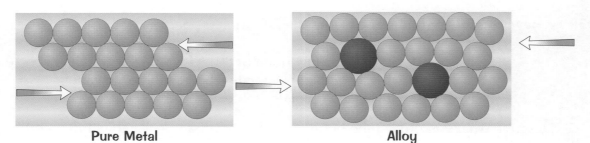

Pure Metal   Alloy

....

....

....

A Wordsearch on Metals

Q1 Fill in the missing letters for the metals below, then search for them in the word search.

Write the letters in the gaps:

A__uminium   Le__d   Po__assium
__alcium   Lith__um   __ilver
Chro__ium   Ma__nesium   __odium
__obalt   Ma__ganese   __in
Co__per   Mercur__   Ti__anium
__old   __ickel   Tun__sten
__ron   Platinu__   __inc
        Zir__onium

```
A  P  L  A  T  I  N  U  M  E  E  S  K
L  O  T  T  T  I  T  A  N  I  U  M  L
U  T  C  R  U  I  G  O  L  D  C  P  E
M  A  N  G  A  N  E  S  E  H  Y  C  K
I  S  I  C  E  M  G  T  L  A  B  O  C
N  S  Z  S  Q  U  H  S  I  F  X  P  I
I  I  I  V  G  I  P  X  T  X  J  P  N
U  U  G  Z  C  M  Y  S  H  E  G  E  V
M  M  U  I  N  O  C  R  I  Z  N  R  I
M  E  R  C  U  R  Y  H  U  L  U  M  O
H  O  U  E  X  H  H  X  M  P  V  G  Z
N  R  M  U  I  C  L  A  C  D  A  E  L
M  U  I  D  O  S  K  Y  G  L  R  E  R
```

Q2 Find a use for five of the metals listed above.

a) ....

b) ....

c) ....

d) ....

e) ....

Questions on Plastic Structures

Q1 Look at the table below which gives information about *plastics*.

Plastic	Cost (£/tonne)	Relative tensile strength	Relative density	Flexibility	Clarity
A	800	1	0.9	Very flexible	Poor
B	4000	10	1.1	Stiff	Good
C	2500	4	1.2	Fairly flexible	Excellent
D	1000	10	1.4	Stiff	Poor
E	1600	8	1.0	Stiff	Good

Which plastic A → E might be good for making the following:

a) a fizzy drink bottle? ....

b) a coat-hanger? ....

c) a 13 amp plug case? ....

d) the case of a transparent watch? ....

e) a shopping bag? ....

f) a breakfast tray? ....

Q2 What information, in addition to that given in the table above, might you need when choosing a plastic for use on the *surface* of the *space shuttle?* Give reasons for your answer.

....

....

....

....

....

Questions on Mixtures

Q1 How is a mixture _different_ from a compound? ....
....
....

Q2 State whether each of the following is an _element_ (**E**), a _mixture_ (**M**) or a _compound_ (**C**).

a) air. ☐	d) iron oxide. ☐	g) distilled water. ☐
b) iron. ☐	e) blood. ☐	h) steel. ☐
c) seawater. ☐	f) common salt. ☐	i) copper. ☐

Q3 In filtration, what is a _filtrate?_ ....

Q4 _Salt cannot be separated from water by filtering._ _Explain_ why. ....
....
....

Q5 What is _decanting?_ ....

Give an _example_ of a mixture that could be separated by decanting. ....
....

Q6 What is the difference between a _solute_ and a _solution?_ ....
....

Q7 How would you _separate_ a solute from a solution _(like salt from seawater)?_ ....
....

Q8 What is a _solvent?_ ....

Q9 What is _crystallisation?_ ....
....

Q10 How could you _separate_ two immiscible liquids? ....
....
....

Questions on Separating Substances

Q1   Which *method* of separation would you use for each of the following:

a) To see if the red colour in rose petals was one colour or a mixture of colours?

....

b) To remove fine traces of sand from seawater so they can be analysed?

....

c) To obtain pure water from seawater?

....

d) To remove traces of yeast from home-made wine?

....

e) To remove chips from chip pan oil?

....

f) To remove alcohol (ethanol) from beer? *(Not that you'd do this of course...)*

....

g) To remove lavender oils from lavender buds?

....

Q2   *Explain* briefly how chromatography works. ....

....

....

....

....

Q3   Look at the chromatogram opposite.

a) Out of A, B, C, D and E, which are:

  i) *mixtures?* ....

  ii) *pure* substances? ....

b) What is <u>C</u> made from? ....

c) What is <u>A</u> made from? ....

A   B   C   D   E

SECTION TWO — CLASSIFYING MATERIALS

Questions on Separating Substances

Q4 Look at the diagram below. _Label_ the fractional distillation apparatus.

Q5 _Explain_ how fractional distillation can separate a mixture of liquids with different boiling points like in crude oil.

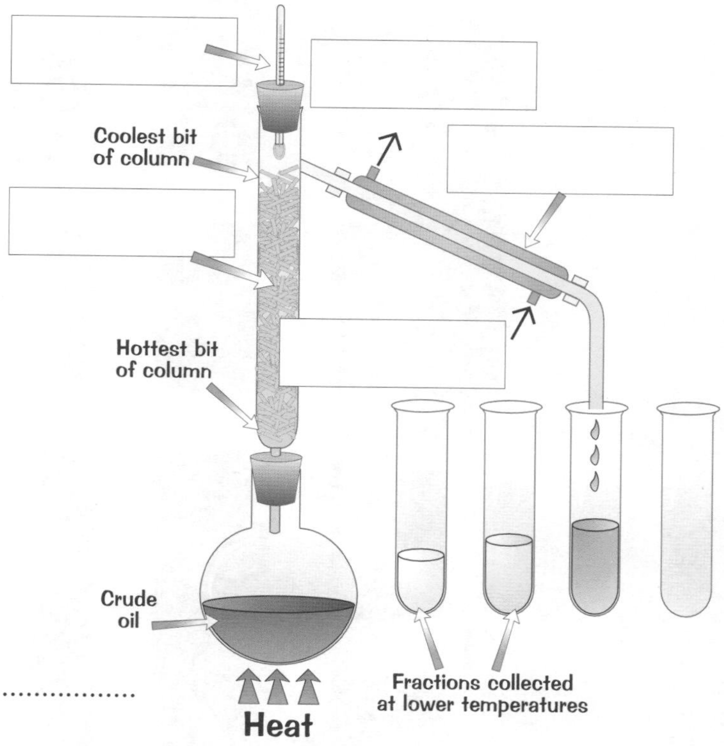

....

....

....

....

....

....

....

....

....

....

....

Coolest bit
of column

Hottest bit
of column

Crude
oil

Heat

Fractions collected
at lower temperatures

Q6 _Link_ the correct separation technique to each mixture below.

Mixture

Separation Technique

Mixture	Separation Technique
Fusel oils (which colour whisky)	Chromatography
Sediments from a soil sample in water	Fractional Distillation
E numbers in sweets	Filter
Port from sediment in the bottle	Centrifugation
Sand and water	Decant
Colours in sweets	Evaporation & Crystallisation
Copper Sulphate in water	
Hydrocarbons in crude oil	
Olive oil and water	

SECTION TWO — CLASSIFYING MATERIALS

Crossword on Section Two

Complete the crossword using the clues below:

Across

1) Substance made of two different elements — it's not a mixture.

4) Lists all the elements in rows and groups.

9) Substances which do not conduct electricity.

10) Substance with all its atoms the same — found in the Periodic Table.

11) Chemical bond formed by transfer of electrons.

12) Type of element found on the left side of the Periodic Table.

13) How you'd separate an insoluble solid from a liquid, like gravel from gravy.

Down

1) How you'd separate lots of dyes in ink.

2) Happens when you melt common salt — it conducts but breaks down.

3) Tiny particle which is the basic building block of all matter — a male cat.

5) Charged atom or group of atoms.

6) Noble gases have it — it's a complete energy level.

7) Structure of water, ammonia and carbon dioxide.

8) Structure of helium, argon and krypton.

Properties of Gases

Q1 *Complete* the table (you may have to think for a while about some parts, and look up others).

Name of Gas	Carbon dioxide	Oxygen	Hydrogen	Ammonia	Chlorine
Formula					
Colour					
Smell					
% in dry air					
Test for the gas					
Soluble in water?					
Boiling point (°C)					
Relative Molecular Mass	44	32	2	17	71
More or less dense than air?					
Two major uses					
Acid or alkali in water?					

Q2 *Describe* in detail how you would identify the above five gases, if they were each given to you in an unlabelled tube. ....

....

....

....

....

....

....

EARTH MATERIALS

Questions on Crude Oil

Read the following text then answer the questions that follow.

Oil and natural gas have formed from the remains of plants and sea creatures. They are the result of the action of heat and pressure on plant and animal remains over millions of years, in the absence of air.

Oil and gas rise up through permeable rocks and become trapped under impermeable rocks, so they can only be extracted by drilling. In the exploration for oil, Geologists carry out test drilling to check for the rock formations that trap oil.

Most wells are 1000 – 5000m deep, but some can reach down 8km. Most of the oil is at high pressure, and so is easily removed. However, some deposits require water to be pumped down to force the oil out. The crude oil is transported in tankers or piped to a refinery where the mixture is separated.

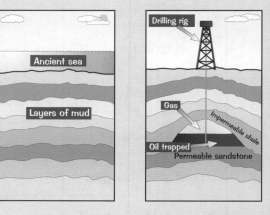

Q1 _Explain_ in your own words how crude oil formed. ....

....

....

....

....

Q2 _Where_ underground does crude oil collect? ....

....

Q3 How is it _extracted (removed)_ from the ground? ....

....

Q4 What does _permeable_ mean? ....

Q5 What does _impermeable_ mean? ....

Q6 What is a _Geologist?_ ....

Questions on Crude Oil

Q7 Where in _Britain_ are _oil deposits_ found? ....

Q8 Where else in the _world_ are _oil deposits_ found? ....

....

Q9 _Oil is a fossil fuel._ What is a _fossil fuel?_ ....

....

Q10 What is a _mixture?_ ....

Q11 Crude oil is a _mixture_ of what? ....

Q12 What is a _hydrocarbon?_ ....

Q13 Why is the oil known as _"crude"_ oil? ....

Q14 _Why_ is crude oil of little use without refining it? ....

....

Q15 Name _two_ methods of transporting crude oil. ....

....

Q16 Why are _oil spills_ a problem to the environment? ....

....

....

Q17 _Oil is non-renewable._ What does this _mean?_ ....

....

Q18 Give two _advantages_ and two _disadvantages_ of burning oil products.

....

....

....

....

....

....

SECTION THREE — EARTH MATERIALS

44

Questions on Coal

Q1   Read the following text then answer the questions below.

Coal began to form over 300 million years ago. At that time much of the Earth was covered by swamp and thick dense forest. As this vegetation died, layer upon layer of decaying organic matter was formed. This changed chemically and was compressed to form rocks.

Coal is found in seams, which are brought near to the Earth's surface by geological changes. Some of these seams can be mined by open-cast methods.

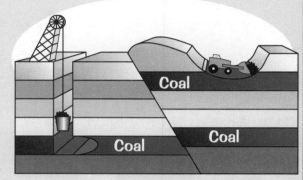

Other seams, which are up to 1 km below the ground, require mining by digging deep shafts.

Coal was used to produce "town gas" before natural gas was more widely used. This was produced by destructive distillation (heating coal without air). Coal can be used to produce many other products, such as coke, dyes, plastics, drugs, weedkillers and even TNT.

a)   What _material_ did the coal form from? ....

b)   _How_ is coal formed? ....

....

c)   What is a _seam?_ ....

....

Q2   What is _shaft mining?_ ....

Q3   What is _open-cast mining?_ ....

....

Q4   What is _destructive distillation?_ ....

....

Q5   What is the difference between _destructive distillation_ and _burning?_ ....

....

....

**SECTION THREE — EARTH MATERIALS**

Questions on Coal

Q6   Give an _advantage_ and one _disadvantage_ of open-cast mining. ....
....
....

Q7   Give an _advantage_ and one _disadvantage_ of shaft mining. ....
....
....

Q8   Coal can be made into coke. What is coke _used_ for? ....
....

Q9   _Coke is cleaner than coal._ _Why_ does it still cause pollution? ....
....
....

Q10   What are the _disadvantages_ of burning coal? ....
....

....

....

Uses of Coal

Q11   _Look at the pie chart._ What is the _major use_ of coal?
....

Q12   _When coal is burnt, carbon dioxide and water (an oxide of hydrogen) are released._

Name another oxide that is produced in large quantities when coal is burned.

....

Q13   What _problem_ does this oxide cause to the environment? ....
....

Q14   _Give_ two uses of coal other than burning it. ....
....
....

Questions on Fractional Distillation

Q1 What is *crude oil?* ....

Q2 What is a *hydrocarbon?* ....

Give an example of a hydrocarbon. ....

Q3 What is a *fossil fuel?* ....

....

Q4 *Complete* the diagram by filling in labels A to E with the correct fraction listed below.

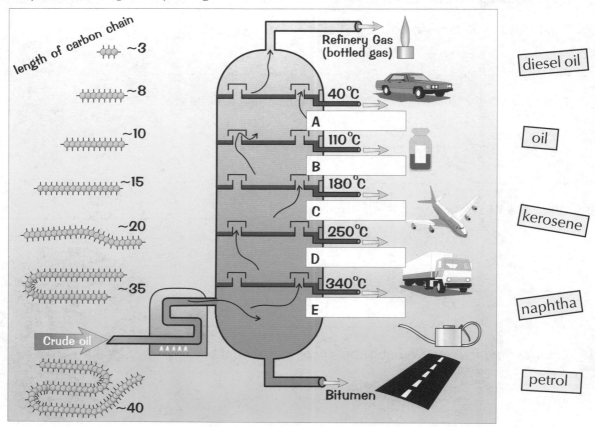

Q5 What do the following terms mean?

a) Volatile: ....

b) Flammable: ....

c) Refining: ....

d) Carbon chain: ....

e) Refinery gas: ....

f) Viscous: ....

g) Distillation: ....

SECTION THREE — EARTH MATERIALS

Questions on Fractional Distillation

Q6   *Describe* the process of fractional distillation of crude oil. ....

....

....

....

Q7   Why is crude oil so *important?* ....

....

Q8   Link up the *first half of the statement* (in grey) with the correct *second half* (in orange).

hydrocarbons become less volatile...

the boiling point of hydrocarbons decrease...

...as the length of the carbon chain increases

hydrocarbon usefulness increases...

hydrocarbons flow less easily...

...as the length of the carbon chain decreases

hydrocarbons become easier to ignite...

hydrocarbons become more flammable...

Q9   *Oil is a finite resource.* What does *finite* mean? ....

....

Q10   What could *you* do to help oil last longer? ....

....

....

Q11   What could *all nations* do to help oil last longer? ....

....

....

Questions on Alkanes

Q1 *Complete the table* by filling in the missing information.

Alkanes $= C_nH_{2n+2}$

Name	Formula	Number of Carbons	Melting Point(°C)	Boiling Point(°C)	Structural Formula
Methane	CH_4	1	-182	-164	H-C-H
Ethane	C_2H_6		-183	-89	H-C-C-H
Propane	C_3H_8	3	-190	-42	H-C-C-C-H
Butane	C_4H_{10}	4	-138	0	H-C-C-C-C-H
Pentane	C_5H_{12}	5	-130	36	H-C-C-C-C-C-H
Hexane		6	-95	69	H-C-C-C-C-C-C-H
Heptane	C_7H_{16}	7	-91	99	H-C-C-C-C-C-C-C-H
Octane		8	-57	126	H-C-C-C-C-C-C-C-C-H
Nonane	C_9H_{20}	9	-51	151	H-C-C-C-C-C-C-C-C-C-H
Decane	$C_{10}H_{22}$		-30	174	H-C-C-C-C-C-C-C-C-C-C-H

Q2 *Draw a graph* on graph paper using the above information, with the number of carbon atoms on the horizontal axis and boiling point on the vertical axis.

Q3 Which alkanes are: **a)** solid **b)** liquid **c)** gas ...at room temperature (20°C)?

....

....

....

Q4 What is the link between the boiling point of alkanes and the number of carbon atoms they

have? ....

Q5 A compound has long, heavy molecules. How will its boiling point be different from a

compound having lighter, shorter molecules? ....

....

Q6 Use your graph to *estimate* the boiling point of $C_{11}H_{24}$. ....

Questions on Alkanes

Q7 Read the text below then answer the questions that follow.

Alkanes are organic compounds that form a family of hydrocarbons. They only contain single covalent bonds and are therefore saturated hydrocarbons. They form 3D molecules but are usually drawn flat. They have the general formula C_nH_{2n+2} (where n is the carbon number). They burn cleanly to produce carbon dioxide and water.

Butane

a) Why are alkanes called *organic* compounds? ....

....

b) *"Saturated"* means that the molecules only contain single covalent bonds. *Explain* what is

meant by a *"single covalent bond"*. ....

....

Q8 State *uses* for methane, propane and butane. ....

....

Q9 Why is it dangerous to burn methane in a limited oxygen supply? ....

....

Q10 *Pure methane has no smell. Below are three molecules used to give methane a smell.*

| $CH_3CH_2 - SH$ | $(CH_3)_3C - SH$ | $CH_3CH_2 - S - CH_2CH_3$ |

Why do you think this is done? ....

....

Q11 *A chemical having the formula $(CH_3)_2CH - SH$ leaked from a university research lab in North Wales. Many local residents complained they could smell natural gas and reported a gas leak. Fishermen even claimed gas could be smelt at sea.*

a) *Explain* why residents reported the smell of natural gas. ....

....

b) Why do you think fishermen could smell the gas *at sea?* ....

....

Questions on Hydrocarbons

If a liquid is quite "thick" and it takes a long time to run down a slope, we say it's "viscous".
We can measure how long it takes for a certain amount of liquid to run through a burette, and
this will indicate how viscous the liquid is.
Lubricating oils in car engines keep moving metal surfaces apart. Viscous oils do this better
than runny oils; but if they are too viscous they don't lubricate the moving parts properly.

The following experiment was set up to find which of two oils was the most viscous.

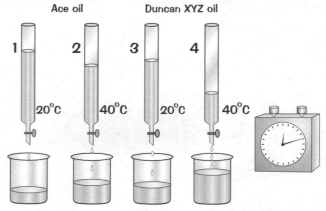

The time taken for the oil to run through the burette was noted at two temperatures.

Burette	Temperature / °C	Time for 50 cm³ of oil to flow through / s
1	20	90
2	40	53
3	20	64
4	40	28

Q1 Draw a bar chart to represent the information in the table above.

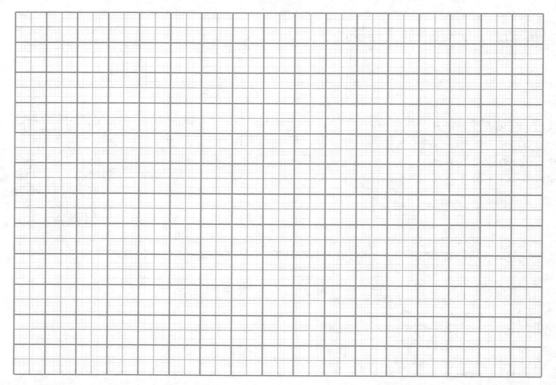

Questions on Hydrocarbons

Use your bar chart to help you answer these questions.

a) Which oil is *most viscous* at 20ºC? ....

b) Which oil is *most viscous* at 40ºC? ....

c) *Temperatures in an engine are much higher than 40˚C.*
What will *happen* to the viscosity of these oils at engine temperature?

....

d) How could you *improve* the experiment to prove which oil was the most viscous when

used in an engine? ....

....

....

Q2 If you were designing an engine oil, would you use *short* chain or *long* chain

hydrocarbons?

....

Q3 What might happen to a *very viscous* oil on a *very cold* morning? ....

....

Q4 *Many years ago, at times when the weather was very cold, lorry drivers would warm their diesel tanks by making a small fire under the tank.*

a) *Why* do you think they did this? ....

....

....

b) What *problems* might occur when doing this? ....

....

....

c) This is not required now as *additives* are put in diesel oil, but not all year round. Why aren't

they *always* put in? ....

....

....

Questions on Polymers and Plastics

Q1   *Explain* what you understand by the term *"polymerisation"*. ....

....

....

....

Q2   *Lots of ethene molecules can join together to form a long chain polymer that is useful.*

$$\underset{H}{\overset{H}{\diagdown}} C = C \underset{H}{\overset{H}{\diagup}} \qquad \underset{H}{\overset{H}{\diagdown}} C = C \underset{H}{\overset{H}{\diagup}} \qquad \underset{H}{\overset{H}{\diagdown}} C = C \underset{H}{\overset{H}{\diagup}}$$

a) What is this useful polymer *called?* ....

b) Using the paper clips below, draw additional paper clips to show how they might link up to represent a chain of molecules.

c) Explain how the paper clip chain above is similar to an ethene polymer. ....

....

....

....

d) *Explain* why ethene's polymer is named the way it is. ....

....

....

e) Write down a use for the polymer of ethene. ....

....

....

Questions on Polymers and Plastics

Q3 Use the information given in the top table to help you complete the second table below.

Plastic	Some properties
1) Polystyrene	Cheap, easily moulded, can be expanded into foam.
2) Polythene	Cheap, strong, easy to mould.
3) Polypropene	Forms strong fibres, highly elastic.
4) PTFE	Hard, waxy, things do not stick to it.
5) Perspex	Transparent, easily moulded, does not easily shatter.

Job	Plastic	Reason
a) Hot food container		
b) Plastic bags		
c) Carpet		
d) Picnic glasses		
e) Buckets		
f) Ropes		
g) Bubble packing		
h) Insulating material		
i) Yoghurt cartons		
j) Non-stick frying pans		

Q4 Sort the following into a list of the *GOOD* and *BAD* points of using plastics.

Can catch fire
Fairly cheap
Moulded easily
Can be very strong
Low density
Difficult to dispose of
Insulators
Non-degradable
Can be coloured
May produce toxic gases when burnt
Not affected by acids or alkalis

Good	Bad

Questions on Metal Ores

Q1   What is a metal *ore?* ....

Q2   *Give* an example of a metal ore. ....

Q3   In what form are very *unreactive* metals found in the ground? ....

....

Q4   *Give two examples* of metals found "native" in the ground. ....

....

....

Q5   In what form are more *reactive metals* found in the ground? ....

....

....

Q6   *The diagram below shows the processes involved in extracting a metal from its ore.*
Match each picture (a → f) with the correct description (1→ 6) from the following box:

1) **Pure metal**	4) **Electrolysis**
2) **Carbon reduction**	5) **Metal ore detected in ground**
3) **Earth containing ore dug from ground**	6) **Waste earth removed to concentrate ore**

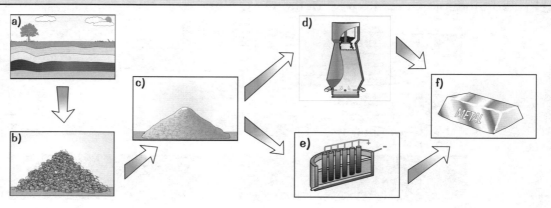

a) = ...   b) = ...   c) = ...   d) = ...   e) = ...   f) = ...

Q7   *When a mining company decides to start mining they must consider a number of issues:*

Place these points (a → d) in order of importance to the mining company.

a) **What amount of metal will be obtained annually?**
b) **What grade is the ore (and how much of it is there)?**
c) **What will be the cost of setting up the mine?**
d) **How much can they sell the metal for?**

1 ....   2 ....   3 ....   4 ....

Questions on Metal Ores

Q8   List each metal in the box under the correct *method of extraction*.

> Iron   Copper   Potassium   Magnesium   Aluminium
>
> Silver   Zinc   Sodium   Lead   Calcium   Gold

Thermal decomposition of ore	Reduction of metal ore with Carbon	Electrolysis of molten ore	Metals that occur naturally

Q9   *Look at the table below.*

a)   Draw a *bar chart* on graph paper showing the abundances of the metals.

Metal	Date first extracted	% Abundance in the Earth's crust
Aluminium	1827	8.1
Calcium	1808	3.6
Copper	Ancient time	<1.0
Gold	Ancient time	<1.0
Iron	Ancient time (Iron age)	5.0
Potassium	1807	2.6

b)   *What does* "abundant" mean? ....

c)   Which is the *most abundant* metal listed? ....

d)   Name a *scarce* metal. ....

e)   What is the relationship between the *reactivity* of the metal and the date it was first

extracted? ....

....

56

Questions on Extracting Iron

Q1   *Iron can be extracted from its ore in a Blast Furnace, which is shown in the diagram.*

   a) List four things that are put into the blast furnace.

....

....

....

....

   b) What is the *name* of the most common iron ore used?

....

   c) Why is *hot air* blasted into the furnace? ....

....

....

Iron ore, coke and limestone

1500°C

Hot air

A   **B**

   d) Why does the temperature need to be as hot as *1500°C?* ....

....

   e) What would you find at *A* and *B* in the diagram? ....

....

Q2   *In the first stage, carbon (as coke) turns into the gas carbon dioxide.*

   Why is carbon dioxide produced? ....

....

....

....

Q3   Carbon monoxide is then produced from the carbon dioxide. Complete the equation

   Carbon dioxide + Carbon   →   _____ _____

                (coke)

Questions on Extracting Iron

Q4   *The final step involves changing the iron oxide into iron by reacting it with carbon monoxide.*

   a) *Complete the word equation* to show what happens.

   Iron oxide + Carbon monoxide → _____ + _____ _____

   b) What has happened to the *iron oxide* in the above reaction? ....

   ....

   c) i) In what *state* is the iron at the end of the reaction? ....

   ii) How is the iron *removed* from the blast furnace? ....

   ....

Q5   *In all chemical processes it is important to remove the impurities, to leave a pure product.*

   a) What is the common name for the main *impurity* mixed with the ore?

   ....

   b) *Calcium carbonate helps to remove this impurity, but first it needs to thermally decompose (breakdown using heat). When this happens, it turns into calcium oxide which then reacts with the impurities to make slag.*

   The equation below shows how slag is formed:

   Calcium oxide + Silicon dioxide → Calcium silicate
              (impurity)   (slag)

   What can this *"slag"* be used for?

   ....

Q6   *Explain why* using the blast furnace makes iron cheaper than a lot of other metals.

   ....

   ....

   ....

   ....

Q7   Give *two* uses of iron. ....

   ....

Questions on Extracting Aluminium

Q1 Use arrows to connect the labels to the corresponding part of the reduction cell.

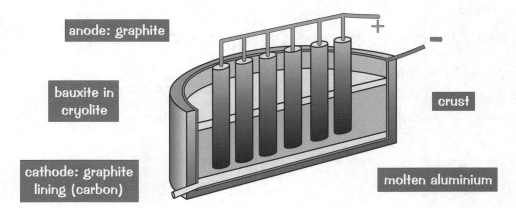

anode: graphite

bauxite in cryolite

crust

cathode: graphite lining (carbon)

molten aluminium

Q2 *Complete* the sentences using the following words:

| reactive | aluminium | ore | difficult |
| oxygen | bauxite | 900°C | cryolite |

Aluminium is much more _____ than carbon so is extracted from its

_____ using electrolysis.

Aluminium is the most abundant metal in the Earth's crust, and is joined up with

other elements, rock and clays, which make it _____ to extract. The ore

of aluminium is called _____ which is impure aluminium oxide. It is

purified, then dissolved in molten _____ *(another ore of aluminium)* which

lowers the melting point from over 2000°C to about _____ °C. Electricity

passes through the melted ore separating the _____ from the oxygen.

The overall equation is: Aluminium oxide → _____ + _____

Q3 Why must the bauxite be *purified* before it undergoes electrolysis? ....

....

Q4 Why is *cryolite* added? ....

....

Q5 Give *two* reasons why adding cryolite is such a good idea. ....

....

Questions on Extracting Aluminium

Q6 *Most countries that mine aluminium do not remove the metal from its ore — they export the ore.* Look at the pie chart and answer these questions:

The Cost of Aluminium

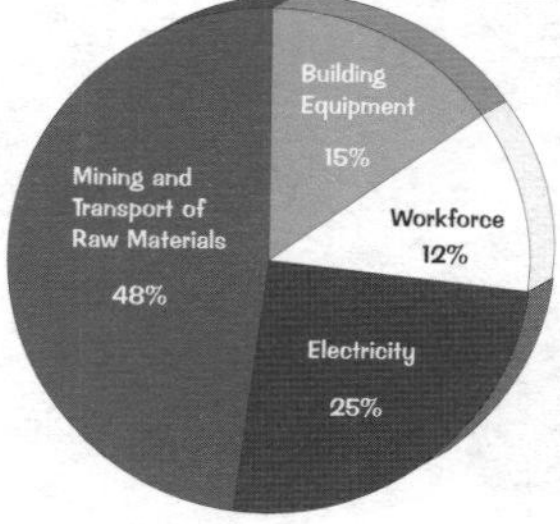

a) Explain why mining and transportation is such a major cost in the production of aluminium. ....

....

b) Give an example of a cheap and convenient way to produce electricity. ....

c) Name two places in the U.K. that might be suitable for producing aluminium.

....

Q7 *A company is considering building an aluminium smelting factory near Fort George.*

Look at the map and list *five features* that make it a suitable site to place an aluminium smelter.

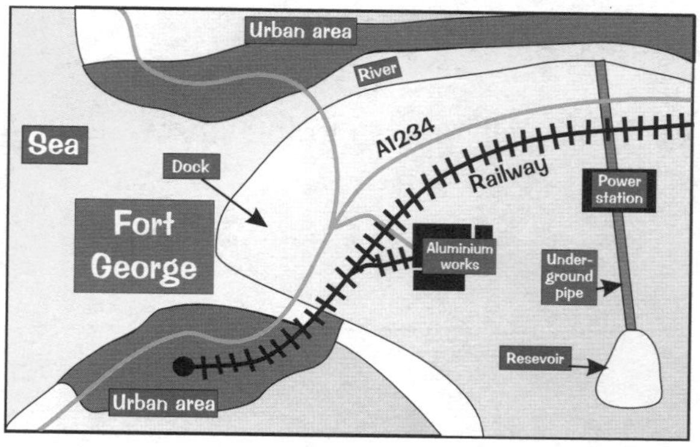

....

....

....

....

Q8 Eight uses of aluminium are illustrated below. Write a correct label next to each picture.

E.g. Milk bottle tops

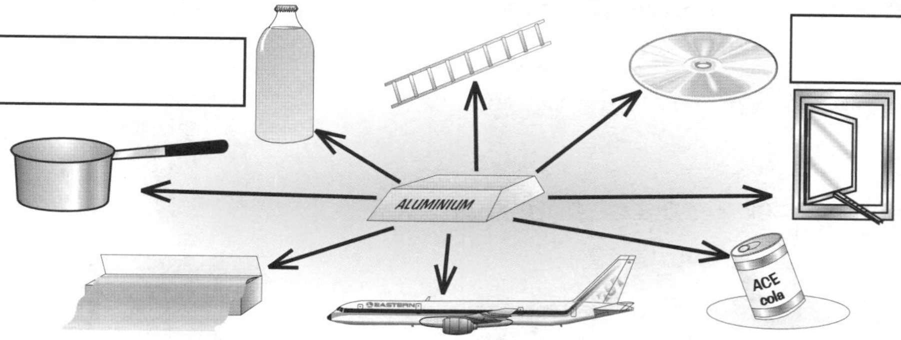

ALUMINIUM

Questions on Copper

Q1   *The common ore of copper is a green substance.*

   a) What is its common *name?* ....

   b) What is the *chemical name* of the ore? ....

Q2   *Copper carbonate can be changed into copper oxide by heating, in a process called* *thermal decomposition. The process is shown in the diagram below.*

   a) What are the bubbles that appear in *Tube 2?*

   ....

   b) What is left in *Tube 1* after the copper carbonate is

   heated? ....

   c) What will happen to the limewater in *Tube 2? Why?*

   ....

   ....

   ....

   d) Write an *equation* for the reaction.

   ....

Q3   *Copper is obtained in the lab from copper oxide by reaction with carbon using the* *apparatus below.*

   a) *Name* apparatus A. ....

   b) *Why* is A heated strongly? ....

   ....

   c) Why does the lid need to be *on* when heating?

   ....

   d) *Explain:*

   i) which element is being *reduced* (losing oxygen).

   ....

   ii) which element is being *oxidised* (gaining oxygen).

   ....

Questions on Copper

Q4 Copper can be purified by electrolysis. *Complete* the following paragraph using the words in the box. *You can use them once, more than once or not at all.*

copper	electricity	anode	negative	attracted	sulphate	positive

Electrolysis is the splitting of a compound by passing _____ through it. It is

used to purify metals. Copper can be purified in this way. Copper _____

solution is the electrolyte — it conducts. It produces copper ions and sulphate ions.

The impure copper is attached to the

_____ electrode, the anode. This

produces copper ions which are attracted

to the _____ cathode.

Here they each gain electrons to become copper metal. A sludge from the impure

copper metal forms underneath the _____.

Q5 Why is copper *more resistant* to corrosion than metals like iron? ....

....

Q6 Why is copper so useful for *electrical wiring* in a house? ....

....

Q7 Give *two* other uses of copper. ....

Q8 Name *two* alloys of copper. ....

Q9 In what *part* of the Periodic Table do you find copper? ....

Q10 Would you expect copper compounds to be *white* or *coloured?* ....

Q11 What *physical property* of copper makes it a suitable material for pans?

....

Q12 *Lithium is a metal that floats on water.*

Does copper float on water? ....

Questions on uses of Metals

Q1

People who badly break a leg or an ankle often have a pin placed in their leg to help the bones heal — they hold the bones in place and add strength to them while they are healing.

The table below lists some materials that could be used to make a pin.

Material	Strength	Reactivity	Cost	Hardness	Density	Toughness
Titanium	H	L	H	H	H	H
Mild Steel	H	H	L	H	H	H
Aluminium	M	M	M	M	M	M
Ceramic	VH	L	L	VH	L	L

L = Low   M = Medium   H = High   VH = Very High

a) Does the pin need to be *strong?* ....

b) Just looking at the strength column — *which example* would you choose for a pin?

....

c) Does the pin need to be *reactive?* ....

d) Just looking at the reactivity column — *which example* would you choose for a pin?

....

e) Does the pin need to be *hard?* ....

f) Just looking at the hardness column — *which example* would you choose for a pin?

....

g) Just looking at the density column — would density affect your decision?

....

h) After examining *ALL* of the information, *explain* in as much detail as possible which

material you would choose for a pin to place in broken bones.

....

....

....

SECTION THREE — EARTH MATERIALS

Questions on uses of Metals

Q2 *The table below lists many properties of metals. <u>Complete</u> the table by filling in for each property two appropriate <u>examples</u> and an <u>exception</u> from the <u>list below</u>, (examples can be used more than once). Then give <u>a use of this property</u> — one has been done for you.*

sodium   lead   silver   aluminium   gold

copper   platinum   cobalt   nickel   tin

lithium   iron   tungsten   titanium

Property (Quality)	Give two examples	Give an exception to rule (if possible)	What is this quality useful for?
Metals are solid	Iron Copper	Mercury	Used in the construction of buildings
Metals are hard (difficult to scratch)			
Metals are strong (have high tensile strength)			
Metals are shiny			
Metals bend			
Metals usually feel cold (conduct heat well)			
Metals conduct electricity well			
Metals are dense (heavy for their size)			
Some metals are magnetic (are attracted to magnetic poles)			
Metals are sonorous (make a nice noise when struck)			
Metals expand when heated			
Metals react with the oxygen in the air			
Metals react with acids			

Questions on Limestone

Q1 What is the name of the main chemical substance in *limestone?*

....

....

Carbonate deposits in England & Wales

North Sea

Millom

Irish Sea

Q2 What *type of rock* is it?
(Igneous/sedimentary/metamorphic)

....

....

Q3 *Name two* other rocks similar in chemical composition to limestone?

....

....

Q4 Name *three* areas shown on the map where there are carbonate deposits.

....

....

Q5 How did the limestone form? ....

....

....

Q6 How do we *remove* limestone from the ground? ....

....

Q7 Why is limestone good to use as a *building material?* ....

....

Q8 Why is limestone used as *road stone?* ....

Q9 When limestone is heated with sand and sodium carbonate it makes which *important*

material? ....

Q10 What new material is formed when limestone is heated with *clay?*

....

Questions on Limestone

Q11 *Mortar is a mixture of calcium hydroxide, sand and water. When the water dries out, the calcium hydroxide reacts with carbon dioxide to make calcium carbonate.*

What *use* does mortar have in the building trade? ....

....

Q12 *Finely ground limestone is used to neutralise acidic soil. How does it neutralise the soil?*

....

Q13 Why do farmers and gardeners often want to *neutralise* soils?

....

Q14 *Limestone is heated on a large scale in rotary kilns like the one shown below. When limestone is heated it thermally decomposes to form calcium oxide.*

a) What does the term *"thermally decompose"* mean? ....

b) Give another name for *calcium oxide*. ....

c) *Describe* what you see when limestone is heated very strongly. ....

....

....

d) What does the expression *"in the limelight"* have to do with limestone?

....

Q15 *The reaction that takes place in the rotary kiln requires heat energy.*

a) What do you call a reaction that *takes in* heat energy? ....

b) *Complete* the equation: (The first letters are given — use the words: *Calcium, carbon, oxide, dioxide.*)

> Calcium carbonate → C_____ o_____ + C_____ d_____

c) Why is the kiln rotated during thermal decomposition? ....

....

Questions on Limestone

Q1 *Calcium hydroxide forms when water is added to calcium oxide.*

Give *another name* for calcium hydroxide. (clue: lasked mile) ....

Q2 *Calcium hydroxide is also used to neutralise farm land.* What *kind of substance* is calcium

hydroxide? ....

Q3 Why does acid rain *damage* limestone buildings? ....

....

....

Q4 *Limestone is a raw material used in the blast furnace — to extract metals like iron.*

What job does limestone do in this extraction process? ....

....

Q5 Fill in the missing letters and then search for the words in the word-search.

Buil_ing		
Ce_ent		
Chal_		
Cla_		
Con_rete		
_lass		
Kil_		
_imelight		
_ar_le		
_ortar		
N_utra_ise		
_uickl_me		
Roa_stone		
S_a_edlime		
_oda		

N	D	J	I	L	V	A	W	D	L	N	M	Y	I
E	H	K	E	A	G	O	T	E	I	D	G	D	Z
U	Q	T	I	V	O	N	S	N	U	F	C	O	K
T	H	G	I	L	E	M	I	L	K	C	I	U	Q
R	W	E	L	M	N	M	I	D	V	D	Q	U	I
A	J	O	E	G	O	R	Y	A	L	C	A	M	S
L	V	C	W	R	T	I	M	H	P	I	E	O	H
I	C	H	T	E	S	T	G	N	P	T	U	A	I
S	L	A	K	E	D	L	I	M	E	L	R	B	D
E	R	L	D	T	A	U	E	R	A	P	L	E	I
D	C	K	S	S	O	D	C	Q	N	R	M	P	E
K	T	U	S	I	R	N	O	S	E	G	B	C	E
W	A	Q	L	H	O	W	P	S	I	N	J	L	Y
S	O	P	E	C	N	T	S	I	Z	C	T	A	E

Questions on the Haber Process

Q1   Why is the Haber Process so *important* in food production? ....
....

Q2   *The two gases used to make ammonia in the Haber Process are hydrogen and nitrogen.*

   a) *Where* does the nitrogen come from?

....

   b) *Where* does the hydrogen come from?

....

Q3   *Look at the diagram opposite — it shows trays of iron catalyst.*

   a) What job does the iron catalyst do?

....
....

   b) What is the *job* of the condenser?

....

   c) At what temperature and pressure is the reaction carried out at? ....

   d) How would a *very low temperature* affect the speed of this reaction? ....

....

   e) *Not all the nitrogen and hydrogen that enters, ends up as ammonia.* This could prove

   expensive — *how* is this problem overcome? ....

....

Diagram labels: Hydrogen · Nitrogen · Gases mix and react · Trays of iron catalyst · Unreacted Nitrogen and Hydrogen · Condenser · Liquid Ammonia
Pressure 200 atmospheres
Temperature 450 °C
Catalyst iron

Q4   *Complete* the following paragraphs by filling in the missing words from the list below. *The words may be used once, more than once or not at all.*

450	1000	ammonia	molecule	hydrogen	nitrogen
200	fertilisers	unreacted	Haber Process	recycled	pressure

_____ is manufactured by the _____ _____ .

One use for ammonia is making _____ . The gases _____ and

_____ are brought together under the special conditions of _____ °C and a

_____ of _____ atmospheres. Nothing is wasted — any _____

hydrogen and nitrogen is _____ .

SECTION THREE — EARTH MATERIALS

68

Questions on Ammonia and Fertilisers

Q1 *Ammonia must undergo a number of reactions in order to produce ammonium compounds. Many of these compounds can act as fertilisers, especially those with the elements nitrogen, phosphorous and potassium.*

What is a fertiliser? ....

Q2 Why are fertilisers so important in the world today? ....

....

Q3 *The production of ammonium compounds like ammonium nitrate is an important part of the nitrogen cycle. Fill in the letter of the missing parts of the cycle in the simplified diagram below.*

| B) Nitrates in the soil |

| D) Nitrogen in the atmosphere |

| A) Plant protein |

| C) Denitrifying bacteria in the soil |

| E) Haber Process |

5 **1** **2** **4** **3** **Ammonium compounds**

Q4 The solubility of ammonium nitrate makes it useful as a fertiliser. Why can this property be

a problem from time to time? ....

....

....

Q5 What does NPK stand for on fertiliser bags? ....

....

Q6 *If the Haber Process stopped and ammonium compounds were not made, what effect would this have on:*

a) the production of *fertilisers?* ....

b) the production of *crops?* ....

SECTION THREE — EARTH MATERIALS

Questions on Ammonia and Fertilisers

Q7   *Plants take up nitrates through their roots to provide themselves with nitrogen.*

a) Why is nitrogen useful to a plant? ....

b) Circle the sentence that best describes how you would notice a plant that *lacked nitrogen.*

A) Yellow leaves with dead bits.

B) Poor root growth and young purple leaves.

C) A small plant with older yellow leaves.

Q8   *Tomato plants were grown in the conditions shown below. All the plants had a constant supply of air and water and were kept at 21°C.*

Which plant is likely to produce *the most* tomatoes? Explain your answer.

....

....

....

....

....

Q9   Fill in the following sentences using the words provided. Each word may be used once or more, or not at all.

Haber	microbes	nitrates	fertilisers	beans	clover
Ammonia	bacteria	nitrogen	nitrifying	nodules	
78%	proteins	fixing	atmosphere	photosynthesis	fixed

An industrial process known as the _____ Process is important because it converts

nitrogen into _____ which is used in making _____ . Nitrogen can

also be _____ by a certain type of plant such as _____ and

_____ . These contain _____ _____

_____ in their roots _____ . Dead plants and animals also put

_____ into the soil. They do this because _____ in their bodies are

broken down by _____ to ammonium compounds. The nitrates are

produced from the ammonium compounds by _____ _____ .

EQUATIONS AND CALCULATIONS

Questions on Redox Reactions

Q1 Reduction and oxidation reactions are often called REDOX reactions. Explain why this is.

....

....

Q2 Tick which is true and which must be false.

	T	F
Oxidation is the loss of oxygen	☐	☐
Oxidation is the gain of oxygen	☐	☐
Reduction is the loss of oxygen	☐	☐
Reduction is the gain of oxygen	☐	☐

Q3 Mark with arrows each of the following reactions to show the oxidation and reduction processes:

Reduction

Copper oxide + Carbon → Copper + Carbon dioxide

$$CuO + C \rightarrow Cu + CO_2$$

Oxidation

a)

Zinc oxide + Carbon → Zinc + Carbon dioxide

$$ZnO + C \rightarrow Zn + CO_2$$

b)

Copper oxide + Hydrogen → Copper + Water

$$CuO + H_2 \rightarrow Cu + H_2O$$

c)

Iron oxide + Carbon monoxide → iron + Carbon dioxide

$$Fe_2O_3 + CO \rightarrow Fe + CO_2$$

Questions on Equations

Q1   *Complete* the following *word* equations — *(remember compounds with two elements end with "–ide").*

a)	Iron	+	sulphur	→	
b)	Iron	+	oxygen	→	
c)	Magnesium	+	oxygen	→	
d)	Sulphur	+	oxygen	→	
e)	Hydrogen	+	oxygen	→	
f)	Magnesium	+	sulphur	→	
g)	Aluminium	+	chlorine	→	
h)	Hydrogen	+	iodine	→	
i)	Carbon	+	oxygen	→	
j)	Iron	+	bromine	→	
k)	Potassium	+	chlorine	→	
l)	Iron	+	sulphur	→	
m)	Lead	+	oxygen	→	
n)	Calcium	+	oxygen	→	

Q2   *Write in* the missing reactants or products formed in the following word equations. Use the following words to fill the gaps.

> zinc   copper   magnesium   hydroxide
> carbon dioxide   copper   sulphuric   carbonate

a) Carbon + Oxygen → ....

b) .... + Sulphuric acid → Zinc sulphate + Hydrogen

c) .... + Chlorine → Copper chloride

d) Hydrogen + Copper oxide → .... + Water

e) Magnesium + ... acid → Magnesium sulphate + Hydrogen

f) .... + Copper sulphate → Copper + Magnesium sulphate

g) Copper .... → Copper oxide + Carbon dioxide

h) Sodium .... + Hydrochloric acid → Sodium chloride + Water

Questions on Relative Formula Mass

Some syllabuses might ask you to: *"Find the mass of one mole of...."*
...Others might ask you to: *"Find the Relative Formula Mass of ...."*

.....They're basically the same thing *(but the first has grams after it).*

Example Question:
Find the mass of one mole of zinc (which is basically the same as asking.... "Find the Relative Formula Mass of Zinc")

*Simply look on the periodic table (at the front of the book) for the relative atomic mass of zinc, which is 65, and add a "g" for grams.
Answer = 65g — yes it's that easy....*

Q1   Find the mass of one mole of each of the following atoms *(find their relative atomic masses).*

    a) calcium (Ca) ....

    b) sodium (Na) ....

    c) iron (Fe) ....

    d) copper (Cu) ....

    e) nitrogen (N) ....

    f) carbon (C) ....

    g) hydrogen (H) ....

    h) chlorine (Cl) ....

    i) potassium (K) ....

    j) lithium (Li) ....

Q2   Find the mass of one mole of each of the following gases *(find their relative formula masses).*

    a) hydrogen (H_2) ....

    ....

    b) oxygen (O_2) ....

    ....

    c) chlorine (Cl_2) ....

    ....

SECTION FOUR — EQUATIONS AND CALCULATIONS

Questions on Relative Formula Mass

Look at the following example for calculating the mass of one mole of a given molecule, then answer the questions below.

Example Question:

Find the mass of one mole of zinc oxide *(which is basically the same as asking.... "Find the Relative Formula Mass of Zinc oxide")*

Simply look on the Periodic Table (at the front of the book) for the relative atomic masses of zinc and oxygen (65 and 16), add them up, and then put a "g" for grams.

Zinc oxide has a formula ZnO. Which contains
$$= (1 \times Zn) + (1 \times O)$$
$$= (1 \times 65) + (1 \times 16)$$
$$= 65 + 16$$
$$= 81g$$

"Find the mass of one mole of...."
which means... *"Find the Relative Formula Mass of ...."*

Q3

    a) copper oxide (CuO) ....

....

....

    b) magnesium oxide (MgO) ....

....

....

    c) potassium iodide (KI) ....

....

....

    d) potassium chloride (KCl) ....

....

....

    e) sodium chloride (NaCl) ....

....

....

Questions on % Element in a Compound

Look at the example below then answer the questions that follow.

Remember this formula:

% Mass of an element in a compound	=	$\dfrac{A_r \times \text{No. of atoms (of that element)} \times 100}{M_r \text{ (of whole compound)}}$

Here is an example worked out for you:

Find the % sodium in Na_2SO_4

$$\frac{A_r \times n \times 100}{M_r} = \frac{23 \times 2 \times 100}{142}$$
$$= \underline{32.4\%}$$

(Remember A_r = Relative Atomic Mass; M_r = Relative Molecular Mass)

Q1 **a)** What is the relative atomic mass (A_r) of carbon (C) = ...

b) What is the relative atomic mass (A_r) of hydrogen (H) = ...

c) Methane (CH_4) has one carbon and four hydrogens in it. Fill in the missing numbers:

 i) The relative mass of one carbon: (1 X C) = (1 x ......)   = ...

 ii) The relative mass of four hydrogens: (4 x H) = (4 x .....)   = ...

 iii) Relative mass of methane (M_r) = (add **i)** and **ii)** N$^{os.}$ up)   = ...

d) What percentage (%) of carbon is there in methane?

$$\% \text{ element} = \frac{A_r \times n \times 100}{M_r}$$

A_r (carbon)   = ...

n (of carbon)   = ...

M_r (of methane) = ...

Put these numbers in the equation...

$$\% \text{ carbon} = \frac{A_r \times n \times 100}{M_r} = \underline{\hspace{4cm}} = ... \%$$

% mass of carbon in methane (CH_4) = ... %

Questions on % Element in a Compound

Q2 Find out:

a) the % carbon in carbon dioxide (CO_2) ....

....

....

....

....

b) the % carbon in carbon monoxide (CO) ....

....

....

....

....

c) the % potassium in potassium chloride (KCl) ....

....

....

....

....

d) the % sodium in sodium fluoride (NaF) ....

....

....

....

....

e) the % copper in copper oxide (CuO) ....

....

....

....

Questions on the Air

Q1 *Copper wire was placed in a tube connected to two gas syringes as shown in the diagram below. The air in the syringes was passed backwards and forwards over the copper as it was heated. After heating for five minutes the apparatus was allowed to cool and the volume of air left in the syringe was noted.*

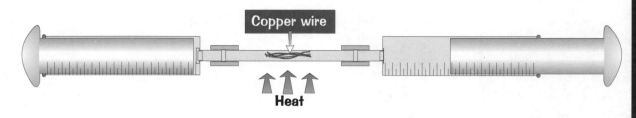

Results.

	Volume of Air	Copper
Start	200cm³	orange
Finish	158cm³	black

a) From the results, *calculate* the reduction in the volume of air. ....
....
....
....

b) *Work this out* as a percentage *(like per 100 cm³)* of air. ....
....

c) What is the name of this *active component* of air, which has apparently disappeared?

....

d) *Where* do you think this active component of air has gone? ....

e) *Construct* a word equation to show exactly what has happened to the copper.
....   + ...   →   ....

f) Why was the apparatus *allowed to cool* before a final reading was taken?

....

g) Name a gas *still present* in the syringes at the end of the experiment and give a *use* for this

gas. ....

Questions on the Atmosphere

Q1   *Stephen set up an experiment to investigate burning. He used four bell jars of different sizes, each having a burning candle on a small dish inside. He discovered that the water rose in all four bell jars.*

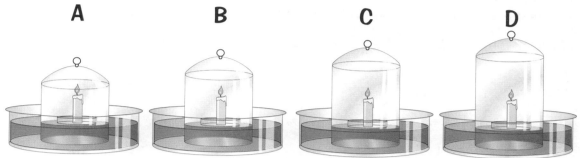

A   **B**   **C**   **D**

a) What gas must be present in the bell jars for the candle to burn properly? ....

b) Why did the water rise? ....

....

....

c) Circle the approximate level the water rose to (as a fraction of the bell jar volume).

    A) 1/2   **B)** 1/3   **C)** 3/4   **D)** 1/5

d) The candle contains hydrogen and carbon — it is a hydrocarbon. What two products will

be made from the complete combustion of the hydrocarbon? ....

....

e) In which bell jar would the candle burn for longest and why? ....

....

Q2   *The three things needed for burning are displayed in the Fire Triangle opposite. Complete the drawing by filling in the two missing labels.*

The Fire Triangle

fuel

Q3   *Incomplete combustion can produce poisonous carbon monoxide. What precautions should be taken in the home to ensure that gas appliances do not produce this gas?*

....

....

SECTION FIVE — AIR AND ROCK

78

Questions on the Greenhouse Effect

Q1 *Many scientists think that the Greenhouse Effect is contributing to global warming. This can happen because greenhouse gases, like carbon dioxide and methane trap infrared radiation inside the atmosphere, which causes it to warm. Higher global temperatures could cause the ice caps to melt — raising the sea levels. With more water about, low-lying areas could flood, while other areas of the world could experience severe droughts.*

Explain using the diagram below how a greenhouse keeps plants warm.

....

....

....

....

....

....

Q2 What keeps the heat *(infrared energy)* in sunlight inside the greenhouse?

....

....

....

....

Q3 *Explain* using the diagram below how the atmosphere can act like a *greenhouse*, causing the planet to warm up, *(the atmosphere is not drawn to scale)*.

....

....

....

....

Q4 What might happen to *global temperatures* if the greenhouse effect continues to intensify?

....

Q5 *Name two* areas in Britain and *two* areas in the rest of the world that are low-lying and would be affected if the sea level rose. ....

....

SECTION FIVE — AIR AND ROCK

Questions on the Greenhouse Effect

Q6 *The table below lists the main contributors to the greenhouse effect.*

a) Label and colour the pie chart to illustrate the data given.

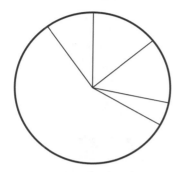

Gas	% Greenhouse Gas
Methane	14
CFCs	14
Nitrogen	5
Carbon dioxide	57
Surface ozone	10

b) Which gas is the *main contributor* to this effect? ....

c) What are humans doing to *increase* the levels of this gas in the atmosphere?

....

d) *Where* might you find a CFC? ....

e) What are the manufacturers of CFCs doing to help *prevent* global warming and damage

to the ozone layer that is caused partly by this gas? ....

....

....

f) *Rotting vegetation adds to the greenhouse effect by producing methane.*

How else might the methane get into the atmosphere? ....

....

Q7 *Look at the table opposite.*

a) What happened in the *early 1800s* to

account for the rise in global temperatures?

....

....

b) *Figures are projected for the years 2050 and 2100.*

What can *we do* to ensure these figures are not achieved? ....

....

Year	Approximate global temperature change
1800	0.0
1850	0.1
1900	0.2
1950	0.5
2000	1.0
2050	2.0
2100	4.0

Questions on Acid Rain

Q1 Read the text below and then answer the questions that follow.

Rainwater is naturally acidic due to carbon dioxide in the atmosphere. This dissolves in water to make a weakly acidic solution.

Carbon dioxide + Water → Carbonic acid

However, combustion of fossil fuels releases pollutants such as sulphur dioxide and oxides of nitrogen into the atmosphere. These also react with rain water and produce even more acidic solutions.

E.g.   **Sulphur dioxide + Water → Sulphurous acid**
(Further oxidation reactions produce sulphuric acid)

At very high temperatures inside a car engine oxides of nitrogen are produced. These are often written as NO_x (because many oxides form). These can form nitric acid on reaction with water making acid rain that falls down to Earth, damaging the environment.

a) Why is rain water *naturally acidic* and which acid does it naturally contain?

....

....

b) What is a *fossil fuel?* ....

....

c) *Name* three fossil fuels. ....

Q2 Give another *name* for combustion. ....

Q3 *Name three* pollutant gases which may be released on combustion of some fossil fuels.

....

....

Q4 *Name two* acids which are not naturally found in rain water.

....

Q5 *What effect* do you think acid rain might have on **a)** fish in lakes **b)** trees in forests?

....

....

Questions on Acid Rain

Q6   *Most of the sulphur dioxide produced worldwide comes from industry and power stations.*

a)   Which fuels do power stations *burn* which unfortunately produce sulphur dioxide?

....

b)   What do you feel they should do to *reduce* the level of this gas in the atmosphere?

....

....

....

Q7   *Power stations now have chemical scrubbers that remove acid gases from the emissions.*

Give the *name* of a type of reaction that will remove the acid gases.

....

Q8   Name a *cheap substance* that could be used to remove these gases. ....

Q9   Natural gas is being used as a fuel in power stations. Give an *advantage* of using gas over

other fossil fuels. ....

Q10   *Road traffic is a major producer of oxides of nitrogen.*

a)   What are most *new* cars in Britain required to have, in order to help *reduce the emission* of

these gases? ....

b)   What other very *harmful* gas is sometimes found in exhaust fumes?

....

c)   *The metals nickel and rhodium can be used to convert carbon monoxide to carbon dioxide*

and the oxides of nitrogen to nitrogen.

Give two *advantages* and *two disadvantages* of using these metals in catalytic converters.

....

....

....

....

Questions on the Rock Cycle

Q1 *Look at the diagram of the rock cycle — its labels are missing.*

a) *Label it* by putting letters from the list below in the white boxes.

A) Metamorphic rocks

B) Transportation

C) Melting

D) Deposition

E) Weathering

F) Burial and compression

G) Igneous rocks

Sedimentary rocks

b) *Explain* how heat and pressure can affect sedimentary rocks. ....

....

....

c) *"Metamorphic rocks form by recrystallisation"*. What is meant by this? ....

....

d) Give *two* examples of ways rocks can be weathered. ....

....

Q2 *The diagram below shows part of the rock cycle.*

a) *Label* parts **(A)** to **(F)**.

(A) .... (B) .... (C) ....

(D) .... (E) .... (F) ....

b) What will happen to the rock in the shaded area **(E)**?

....

c) What type of rock would you find at **(E)**?

....

d) *What difference* would you see in the structure of the rocks formed at **(F)** and those

formed at **(D)**? ....

....

Questions on the Rock Cycle

Q3   *Complete* the following paragraphs by filling in the missing words from the list:

> buried   igneous   metamorphic   weathered   compressed   heat
> melted   magma   sedimentary   millions   sedimentary   metamorphic
> magma   sea   volcano   erupts   rock cycle

Over _____ of years rocks change from one form to another. This is called the

_____ _____. The three main rock types are _____,

_____ and igneous. Rock particles find their way into the

_____ because they are _____ and transported by wind

and water. Over millions of years these become buried and _____, and

form _____ rock. Sometimes these rocks become _____ deeper

into the Earth, and are changed by _____ and pressure into

_____ rocks. Metamorphic rock can be buried still further where, completely

_____, it becomes _____. Pressure forces the _____

upwards where it either _____ as a _____ or goes into existing

cracks in rock, forming _____ rock.

Q4   Label the diagram with the following words. The first one, **A**, has been done for you.

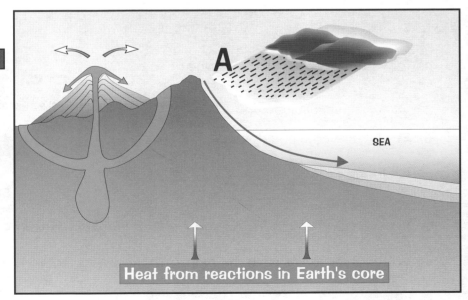

A - weathering
B - heat and pressure
C - melting
D - compression
E - burial
F - recrystallisation
G - eruption
H - deposition
I - transport

SEA

Heat from reactions in Earth's core

Questions on Sedimentary Rocks

Q1   *Most sedimentary rocks form on continental shelves surrounding land masses. Weathered material is transported to the shelves to form successive beds or strata.*

a)   *Explain* what happens when pressure is applied to a layer of sediment.

....

b)   Cement holds pieces of sedimentary rock together. *Explain* how this forms?

....

....

c)   Why are *fossils* found in sedimentary rocks but not in igneous or metamorphic rock?

....

....

....

d)   *Plant and animal remains decay in sedimentary rock to make a useful substance.*

Name this useful substance. ....

Q2   *Sedimentary rocks are fragments of other rocks found in a natural cement.*

Explain how the rock fragments can be identified.

....

....

....

Q3   *Look at the diagram.* Answer the following questions by writing A, B, C, D or E.

a)   In which layer(s) could *limestone* be found?

....

b)   In which layer(s) could *marble*

be found? ....

c)   In which layer(s) would you find the *least number of fossils?* ....

d)   Which layer A → E is: **i)** the *oldest,* **ii)** the *youngest?*

i) ....   ii)...

SECTION FIVE — AIR AND ROCK

Questions on Sedimentary Rocks

Q4   *Match* the rocks with the correct descriptions below by drawing arrows between them.

a) Limestone

b) Shale

c) Conglomerate

d) Sandstone

i) Formed from fine particles grey in colour. Will easily split into layers.

ii) Pebbles and chips of rock in a cement.

iii) Made from sand. Particles stuck together.

iv) Formed from shells, mostly calcium carbonate, grey/white colour.

Q5   *Earth movements cause layers of sedimentary rock to move. An example is shown in the diagram below:*

a)   How can you tell that the Earth's crust has *moved?* ....

....

....

b)   What is this formation *called?* ....

Q6   Fill in the following paragraph using the words provided.

| metamorphic | crystallise | cement | fossils | destroyed | water |
| pressure | cements | melt | sedimentary | magma | |

Sedimentary rocks contain _____ which will not be present in igneous

or metamorphic rocks because they would have been _____ .

Sedimentary rocks contain a natural _____ which is made because

_____ squeezes the _____ out and salts

_____ , which _____ particles together.

Metamorphic rocks are formed when _____ rocks are heated

and compressed. The sedimentary rock does not _____ or

_____ would be formed and not _____ rock.

SECTION FIVE — AIR AND ROCK

Questions on Igneous Rocks

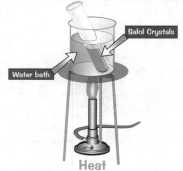

Q1 *The size of an igneous rock's crystal depends on the rock's rate of cooling when it was being formed. It is possible to set up an experiment in the lab using salol to investigate the relationship between crystal size and rate of cooling. In the apparatus shown opposite, the salol melts to form a clear liquid, which can then be removed and recrystallised.*

a) Why is it better to use a *water bath* than to directly heat the

crystals over a Bunsen burner? ....

....

....

b) *Explain* a method you could use to ensure that:

i) the salol cooled quickly ....

....

ii) the salol cooled slowly ....

....

c) Which would give the *larger* crystals, results from experiment **b) i)** or from **b) ii)**?

....

Q2 *In some igneous rocks the crystals are visible and in some they are not.*

a) Where do some igneous rocks cool to give *small* crystals? ....

....

b) Where do some igneous rocks cool to give *large* crystals? ....

....

Q3 *Use the letters A) → D) to label* the diagram below to indicate where you would find:

A) *Extrusive* igneous rock.

B) *Intrusive* igneous rock.

C) *Magma.*

D) *Lava.*

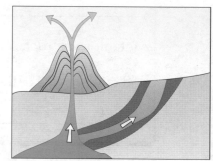

Q4 Name *one* intrusive and *one* extrusive igneous rock.

.... and ....

Questions on Igneous Rocks

Q5 *The diagram below shows a piece of igneous rock amongst layers of sedimentary rock.*

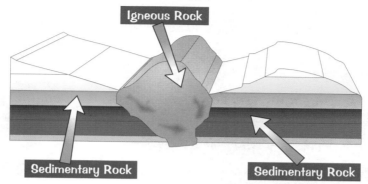

Igneous Rock

Sedimentary Rock

Sedimentary Rock

a) *Explain* how the igneous rock came to be there. ....

....

....

b) *Explain* why in a few thousand years this lump of igneous rock may stand well above the

rest of the landscape. ....

....

....

....

Q6 Sometimes igneous rock, such as pumice, can be very light and have holes in it.
Explain how pumice is formed and why it has this form.

....

....

....

....

Q7 *Complete* the following sentences using the correct words from the list below.

volcano	intrusive	magma	small	large	extrusive	erupts

a) _____ igneous rocks cool slowly and have _____ crystals.

_____ cools in existing cracks in rock.

b) _____ igneous rocks cool quickly and have _____ crystals.

Lava _____ out of a _____ and cools outside the Earth.

Questions on Metamorphic Rocks

Q1   What does *metamorphic* mean? ....

Q2   What causes rocks *underground* to be subjected to large forces? ....

....

Q3   *The diagram below shows a section of the rock cycle where metamorphic rocks form.*

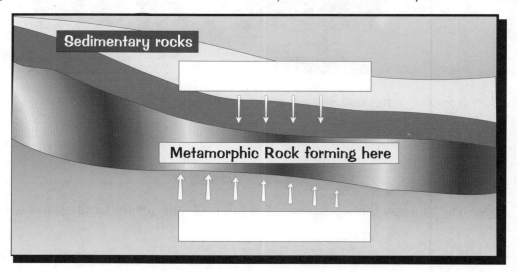

a)   *Write* on the diagram in the correct white box:

    i) where *pressure* acts.

    ii) where *heat* comes from.

b)   Why do sedimentary rocks *recrystallise* to form metamorphic rocks? ....

....

c)   Where in the diagram might *magma* be formed? ....

d)   Where does the *heat* come from to cause rock changes? ....

....

Q4   Draw arrows to *match up* the rock types with the correct descriptions.

Grey, can be split into layers

Marble

Layers of crystals,

including dark mica

Slate

Small sugary crystals,

white/grey in colour

Schist

Questions on Metamorphic Rocks

Q5 *Slate and schist are different but both form from mudstone and shale.* What causes the *difference* between them? ....

....

....

....

Q6 *People grow crops near volcanic areas even though there are risks of volcanic eruptions.* Explain why the soil there is *so fertile.* ....

....

....

....

....

Q7 *Complete* the table by giving uses for the various types of rock.

Rock	Use
Sandstone	
Limestone	
Slate	
Marble	

Why are metamorphic rocks generally *harder* and *more resistant to erosion* than sedimentary rocks? ....

....

....

....

A Summary of Rock Types

Q1 *Match* the rock name to the correct rock type by drawing arrows between them.

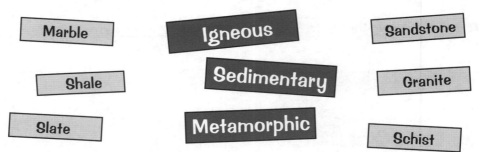

Marble   Igneous   Sandstone

Shale   Sedimentary   Granite

Slate   Metamorphic   Schist

Q2 *Look at the diagrams below that show different types of rocks.*

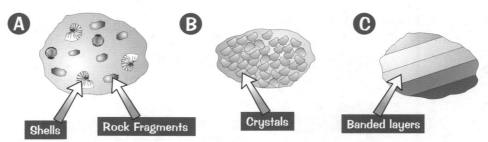

A — Shells, Rock Fragments
B — Crystals
C — Banded layers

a) For each of A, B and C, state whether it is an igneous, a sedimentary or a metamorphic rock. *Give a reason* for your choice in each case.

A) .... , reason: ....

B) .... , reason: ....

C) .... , reason: ....

b) *Name* an example of each of these type of rocks. ....

....

Q3 *Complete* the following sentences using the correct words from the list below.

> heat   sedimentary   heated   melt   texture
> injection   metamorphic   Earth   pressure

_____ rocks are changed into _____ rock

by _____ and _____ . _____ movements

push rocks underground. The _____ of metamorphic rocks is changed

but the rocks do not _____ . If they did, they would not be

metamorphic rocks. Metamorphic rocks can also form when an _____ of

magma in cracks in existing rocks causes the rock around to be _____ .

An Earth Science Crossword

Complete the crossword using the clues below. Some letters have been given to help you get started.

Across

1) Most dense type of tectonic plate (7,5)
4) Igneous rocks that form on the surface of the Earth (9)
6) Scale used to measure earthquake intensity (6,5)
10) Energy source which drives the rock cycle on the surface of the Earth (3)
11) Often seen when two continental plates collide (9)
12) Type of plate margin where one plate dips beneath the other (11)
14) Type of decay that creates the Earth's heat (11)
17) Rock containing layers of fine particles (11)
18) Common carbonate rock (9)

Down

2) Type of plate margin where new rocks are formed (12)
3) Rock type formed from molten magma (7)
4) Often experienced on the San Andreas Fault (11)
5) Layer of the Earth about 35km thick (5)
7) Currents which cause plate movement (10)
8) Igneous rocks that form inside the Earth (9)
9) State of the outer core (6)
11) Rocks formed by the action of heat and pressure on sedimentary rocks (11)
13) All the continents were originally joined up to make this (7)
15) Example of an igneous rock (6)
16) Centre of the Earth (4)

Questions on the Water Cycle

Q1   *The water cycle has four distinct parts.* Use the words in the box to *label* the diagram.

Evaporation
Precipitation
Runoff
Storage

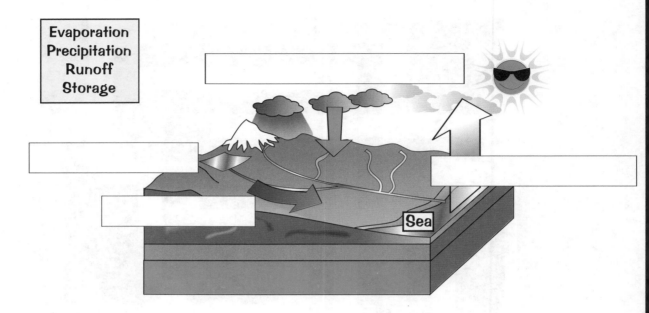

Sea

Q2   Why is the water cycle known as a *"cycle"?* ....
....

Q3   *Name three* places in Britain where water might be stored on land. ....
....

Q4   *Name* the world's two main reservoirs of fresh water. ....
....

Q5   *How* does water get to the sea? ....
....
....

Q6   What is the *energy source* for the water cycle? ....

Q7   What is *transpiration?* ....

Q8   Where in the world does the *most transpiration* occur? ....

Q9   What does the water vapour *form* after it has evaporated? ....

Q10   *When water vapour rises into the atmosphere it cools and turns into a fine mist of water.*

    What is the *name* given to this physical process? ....

Questions on the Water Cycle

Q11 Name *three types* of precipitation. ....

....

Q12 *Where in the world* do you think *74%* of the total precipitation falls?

....

Q13 *Where in the world* do you think *84%* of the total evaporation occurs?

....

Q14 Name two *weather conditions* that would increase the rate of evaporation.

....

Q15 Why is the water cycle so *important?* ....

....

....

Q16 *Water vapour is a greenhouse gas.* What does this *mean?* ....

....

Q17 Does *human activity* have much effect on the amount of water in the atmosphere?

....

Q18 Starting in an ocean, *describe* the journey of a water particle around the water cycle.

....

....

....

....

Q19 Look at the diagram below. In what way is this diagram

similar to the water cycle? ....

....

....

....

Questions on Weathering and Erosion

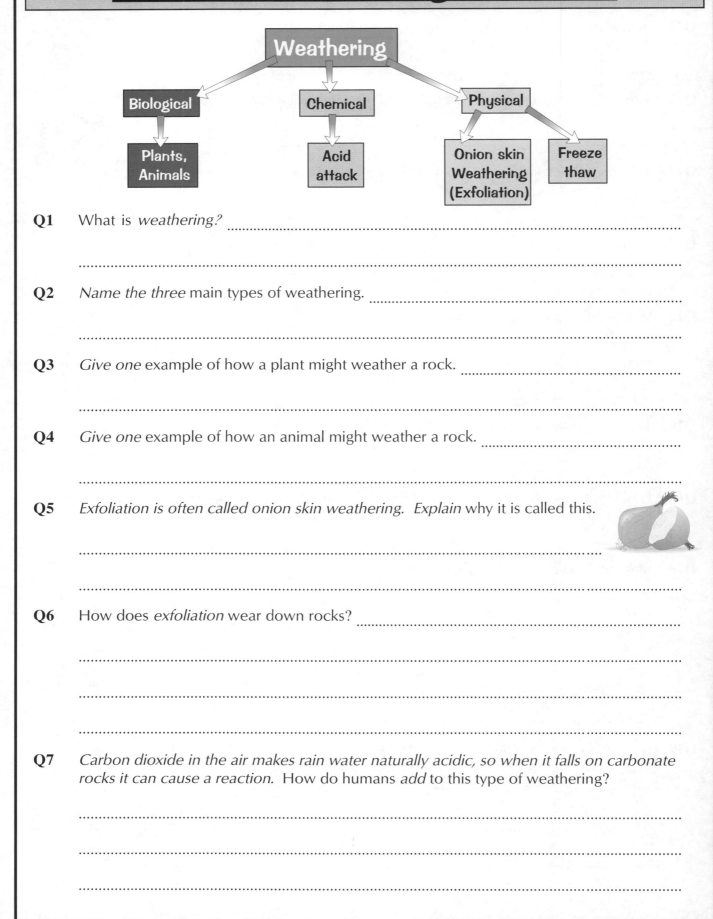

Q1 What is *weathering?* ....
....

Q2 *Name the three* main types of weathering. ....
....

Q3 *Give one* example of how a plant might weather a rock. ....
....

Q4 *Give one* example of how an animal might weather a rock. ....
....

Q5 *Exfoliation is often called onion skin weathering. Explain* why it is called this.
....
....

Q6 How does *exfoliation* wear down rocks? ....
....
....
....

Q7 *Carbon dioxide in the air makes rain water naturally acidic, so when it falls on carbonate rocks it can cause a reaction.* How do humans *add* to this type of weathering?
....
....
....

Questions on Weathering and Erosion

Q8 *A student placed a glass sample tube full of water in a freezer over night. In the morning the tube was cracked.*

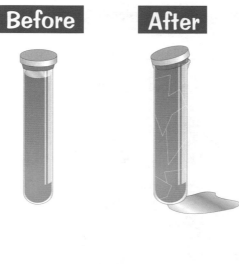

Before   **After**

a) Why did the tube crack? ....

....

b) How can the results help us to *explain* freeze-thaw weathering? ....

....

....

Q9 Which of the three main rock types is generally the *easiest* to weather?

....

Q10 *When rocks have been weathered they often form fine sediment that is transported by wind or water. Name three ways in which water might carry away the sediment.*

....

....

Q11 What is *erosion* and which processes does it include? ....

....

....

....

Q12 *Sedimentary rocks are formed from the sediment that is made by erosion.*

What other vitally important *substance* is made from erosion? ....

....

Questions on the Earth's Structure

Q1   Approximately *what proportion* of the Earth's surface is covered by water? ....

Q2   Why is the Earth known as the *blue* planet? ....

....

Q3   *Name* the three main layers within the Earth. ....

....

Q4   *Complete* the diagram below by labelling the three layers you named in question 3.

....

....

....

Q5   *Link up* the name with the correct depth, state and composition in the diagram below.

Name	Depth	State	Composition
Mantle	2,225 km	solid	iron and nickel
Inner core	20-35Km	dense liquid	iron / magnesium silicates
Outer core	2,900 km	rock that can flow due to high forces	iron and nickel
Crust	1,275 km	solid rock	oxygen, silicon, aluminium

Q6   *The temperature rises as you go deeper into the Earth. This is because heat is produced inside the Earth by radioactive decay.*

   a) What does the term *"radioactive"* mean? ....

....

   b) Why doesn't the Earth *cool down* from radiation loss, like a kettle of hot water would?

....

....

....

SECTION FIVE — AIR AND ROCK

Questions on the Earth's Structure

Q7   Convection currents form inside the Earth as result of radioactive decay.

What do these *convection currents* cause? ....

Q8   *Name* the two types of crust. ....

Q9   Why does the crust *float* and not *sink* into the mantle below it? ....

....

....

....

Q10   *The Earth's crust is divided into about a dozen continental plates.*

Give another *name* for continental plates. ....

Q11   *Look at the table showing the abundance of various elements in the Earth's crust.*

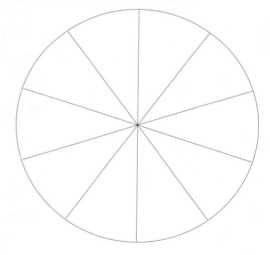

Element	% by mass in Earth's crust
Oxygen	50
Silicon	26
Aluminium	7
Iron	4
Calcium	3
Potassium	2.5
Sodium	2.5
Magnesium	2
Hydrogen	1
Other	2

a) Put this information into the *pie chart.*

b) Which is the *most abundant (most common)* metal? ....

c) Which is the *most abundant* non-metal? ....

d) Are all these elements found as *pure elements* in the Earth's crust? ....

e) *Aluminium costs about three times as much as iron to buy.*

Why do you think this is? ....

....

....

Questions on Plate Tectonics

Read the following passage and look at the diagram below about plate movements.

> The Earth is cracked into a number of large pieces called tectonic plates. These move slowly due to convection currents in the hot viscous mantle of the Earth. The plates move only a few centimetres a year but when they press against each other, huge forces are exerted upon rocks, causing mountains ranges to form (over millions of years). Sediment beds are also pushed into folds. Some tectonic plates are moving away from each other. We know this because they have: i) similar shapes and could fit together like a jigsaw and ii) similar patterns of rocks and fossils.

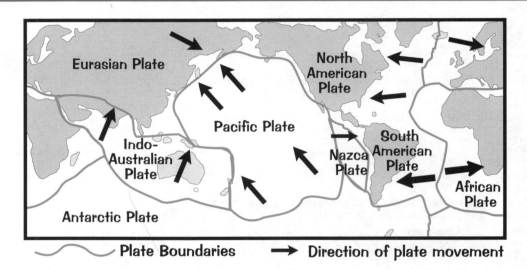

Plate Boundaries ⟶ Direction of plate movement

Q1   What are the *large pieces* of crust known as? ....

Q2   What causes plates to *move*? ....

....

Q3   *Explain* what colliding plates moving together can give rise to. ....

Q4   *Name* two pieces of evidence that supports the theory of tectonic plate movement.

....

....

....

....

....

Q5   What is the name of the plate *Britain* is on? ....

....

Questions on Plate Tectonics

Q6 *Look at the picture below which shows layers of sediment in part of the Earth's crust.*

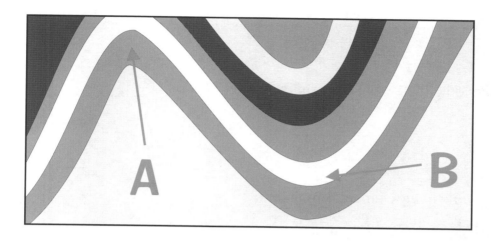

a) What is this *formation* known as? ....

b) What does *each* feature A and B represent?

A) .... B) ....

c) How can these formations be *produced*? ....

....

....

d) *Crust movements can put large amounts of rock under huge amounts of strain.* When this

strain is *released*, what is usually experienced? ....

....

Q7 *The map shows the two continents South America and Africa. The line between them shows where a plate boundary occurs.*

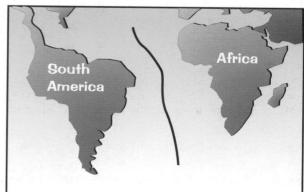

a) *Draw an arrow* on each continent to show its direction of motion.

b) What do you notice about the *shapes* of the two continents that suggests they have been in contact in the past? ....

....

SECTION FIVE — AIR AND ROCK

PATTERNS OF BEHAVIOUR

Questions on the Periodic Table

Q1 In the Periodic Table what is meant by the term *Group?* ....

....

....

Q2 In the Periodic Table what is meant by the term *Period?* ....

....

....

Q3 Roughly *how many* elements are there? ....

Q4 In what *order* are the elements listed in the Periodic Table? ....

....

Q5 How is this different from the very first attempt at listing elements in the Periodic Table?

....

....

....

....

....

Q6 What might be *similar* about members of the same group? ....

....

....

Q7 What might be *similar* about members of the same period? ....

....

....

Q8 Whose *idea* was it to put the elements in this order? ....

Q9 On which side of the Periodic Table would you find the metals? ....

Q10 On which side of the Periodic Table would you find the non-metals? ....

Questions on the Periodic Table

Q11 In this Periodic Table some elements are shown as letters:

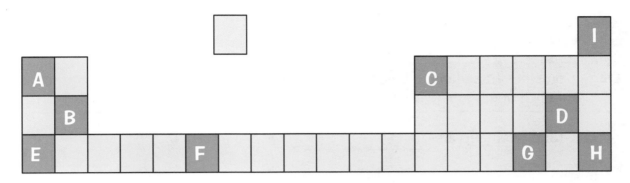

These letters are NOT the proper symbols for the elements.

Use the appropriate letter(s) from the above Periodic Table to answer each of the following questions:

WHICH ELEMENT...

a) is a Noble gas? ....

b) is a Halogen? ....

c) is in Group II? ....

d) is in the same period as D? ....

e) has an atomic number of 3? ....

f) are the least reactive non-metals? ....

g) is a transition element? ....

h) has a mass number of 39? ....

i) will have the highest melting point? ....

j) is in Period 1? ....

k) will have ions that carry a 1^+ charge? ....

l) will have ions that carry a 1^- charge? ....

m) has three electrons in its outer shell? ....

n) may form a coloured compound? ....

General Questions on The Periodic Table

Q1   List all the members of Group I.

....

....

Q2   Complete the sentences below about *Group I* elements by choosing the correct word(s) for each one.

a) Group I elements are _____ . *(metals/non-metals)*

b) They are all _____ substances with a _____ density. *(hard/soft, high/low)*

c) They are all very _____ and are kept in a bottle of _____ .

(reactive/unreactive, oil/water)

d) They tarnish _____ in air. *(easily/with difficulty)*

e) They become _____ reactive going down the Group. *(more/less)*

f) A typical member of the Group is _____ . *(calcium/sodium)*

g) They form _____ ions. *(1^+ / 1^-)*

Q3   List all the members of Group 7.

....

....

Q4   Select the correct words to describe *Group 7* elements.

a) All the Group VII elements are _____ . *(metallic/non-metallic)*

b) They are all _____ of electricity. *(conductors/non-conductors)*

c) Their melting points _____ going down the Group. *(increase/decrease)*

d) Chlorine is a _____ at room temperature. *(solid/liquid/gas)*

e) Bromine is a _____ at room temperature. *(solid/liquid/gas)*

f) Iodine is a _____ at room temperature. *(solid/liquid/gas)*

g) Chlorine, Bromine and Iodine get _____ in colour going down the Group.

(lighter/darker)

h) They form _____ ions. *(1^+ / 1^-)*

SECTION SIX — PATTERNS OF BEHAVIOUR

General Questions on The Periodic Table

Q5 Many Periodic Tables have a *zig-zag* line on them.

What two types of element does this line *divide?*

....

Q6 *Where* are the *metals* in the Periodic Table in relation to this line?

....

Q7 *Where* are the *non-metals* in the Periodic Table in relation to this line?

....

Q8 Some elements are known as *semi-metals* or *metalloids*.

a) *Where* are these elements found in the Periodic Table?

....

b) Give *one example* of a *semi-metal* element.

....

Q9 One element is *unlike* any other as it is *not* shown as a member of any group.

Name this element. ....

Q10 Where are the *transition metals* found on the Periodic Table?

....

Q11 Which is the most reactive member of Group I? ....

Q12 Which is the most reactive member of Group II? ....

Q13 Sodium has an atomic number of 11 and a mass number of 23.

Explain in as much detail as possible what this tells us about an atom of sodium.

....

....

....

....

....

Questions on Group 0 — The Noble Gases

Q1　Why are the Noble gases sometimes known as *Group VIII (Group 8)* elements?

....

Q2　*The Noble gases are "inert".* What does this mean in science? *(Circle one from the following.)*

A) They are very reactive.　　　　　　　　**B)** They are very unreactive.

C) They react with some things but not others.　**D)** Lackadaisical.

Q3　Use the table to *answer* these questions:

	Hydrogen	Helium
Structure of Atom	(H) x	(He) x
Boiling Point °C	-253	-269
Melting Point °C	-259	-272
Atomic Number	1	2
Mass Number	2	4

a) Is helium a solid, a liquid, or a gas, at a temperature of 20°C? ....

b) How many electrons do hydrogen and helium atoms have in their outer shells (energy levels)?

Hydrogen has _____ electrons in its outer shell.

Helium has _____ electrons in it outer shell.

c) Elements react to gain a full outer shell. Out of hydrogen and helium which is the most

reactive? ....

d) Why is helium now used in airships rather than hydrogen?

....

....

....

Q4　*The density of dry air is 0.0013 g/cm³. The density of helium is 0.00017 g/cm³ and the density of argon is 0.0016 g/cm³.*

Why is helium used in *meteorological balloons*, rather than argon?

....

....

....

Questions on Group O — The Noble Gases

Q5 *The table below gives information about the Noble gases. Use it to answer the questions that follow.*

Noble Gas	Atomic Number	Density at STP g/cm³	Melting Point °C	Boiling Point °C
Helium	2	0.00017	-272	-269
Neon	10	0.00084	-248	-246
Argon	18	0.0016	-189	-186
Krypton	36	0.0034	-157	-153
Xenon	54	0.006	-112	-107
Radon	86	0.01	-71	-62

a) How do the *melting and boiling points* of the gases change as you go down the group?

....

b) How do the *densities* of the Noble gases change as you go down the group?

....

c) Why is neon used in *advertising signs?* ....

....

Neon is Ace!

d) Give another *use* of neon. ....

....

Q6 *Complete the paragraph below from the word list. Words can be used once, more than once, or not at all.*

Periodic	inert	1%	Noble	increase	shell
low	helium	argon	neon	radioactive	O

The _____ gases are found in Group _____ in the _____

Table. They are called Noble gases because they do not react with any other element,

because they have a full outer _____ of electrons orbiting the nucleus.

They are also called the _____ gases. The Noble gases have very

_____ boiling points which _____ down the group. The

Noble gas with the largest atoms is radon and the one with the smallest atoms is

_____ . About _____ of the air is made up of Noble gases.

Questions on Group I — The Alkali Metals

Q1 Draw arrows to match up the alkali metals to the correct descriptions of their reactions in water.

A) Potassium	1) Ignites with yellow/orange flame, fizzes vigorously.
B) Sodium	2) No flame, but fizzes.
C) Lithium	3) Pops and ignites with a lilac flame, fizzes very vigorously.

Q2 Put the metals in the box in order of their reactivity — the most reactive first.

Caesium

Potassium

Lithium

Sodium

Rubidium

1) ....

2) ....

3) ....

4) ....

5) ....

Q3 *When an alkali metal reacts with water, a gas and a colourless solution is produced.*

a) *Name* the gas that is produced. ....

b) How could you test for this gas? ....

....

c) What *colour* would the resulting colourless solution change to if universal indicator was

added? ....

d) What would be the *pH* of the resulting solution?

A) 1-3   B) 4-7   C) 8-9   D) 9-11   Answer = ...

Q4 *Complete* the table below using the three sentences provided.

i) Tarnishes quickly to give an oxide layer.
ii) Tarnishes slowly to give an oxide layer.
iii) Tarnishes very quickly to give an oxide layer.

	Reaction of the Metal in Air
Lithium	
Sodium	
Potassium	

SECTION SIX — PATTERNS OF BEHAVIOUR

Questions on Group I — The Alkali Metals

Q5   Explain why a freshly cut piece of sodium would have a shiny surface, but after a while it

would turn white. ....

....

....

Q6   *Group I of the Periodic Table is known as the Alkali Metals.*

a) Why is Group I of the Periodic Table known as the *Alkali Metals?* ....

....

....

b) Why are they known as *"Group I"* in the Periodic Table? ....

....

....

Q7   How are the Alkali metals *stored* and why are they stored this way?

....

....

....

Q8   *The table below shows four alkali metals and some of their physical properties.*

Alkali Metal	Atomic Mass	Symbol	Boiling Point °C	Melting Point °C	Density g/cm³
Lithium	7		1342	181	0.535
Sodium	23		880	98	0.971
Potassium	39		760	63	0.862
Rubidium	85.5		688	39	1.53

a) Complete the table by filling in the *symbol* column.

b) In what way do the boiling and melting points change as you go down the group?

....

....

c) Which of the alkali metals listed is the most dense? ....

Questions on Group VII — The Halogens

Q1   Why are the halogens known as the Group VII elements? ....

....

Q2   *Look at the information in the table.*

Halogen	Melting Point °C	Boiling Point °C
Fluorine	-220	-188
Chlorine	-101	-35
Bromine	-7	58
Iodine	114	184

What is the trend found for the melting and boiling points as you go down the group?

....

....

Q3   Use the information above to help you *complete* the table below.

Halogen	Number of electrons in outer shell	State at room temperature	Colour at room temperature	Symbol
Fluorine	7			
Chlorine		gas		
Bromine			brown	
Iodine				I

a)   Bromine is a brown volatile liquid. What is meant by *volatile?* ....

....

b)   How does the *reactivity* change as you go down the group? ....

....

....

Q4   Halogens react with metals to make salts like sodium chloride (common salt). What type of bonding is found in these types of compounds?

    A) ionic

    B) metallic

    C) covalent   Answer = ...

    D) ionovalent

Questions on Group VII — The Halogens

Q5 Halides form from halogens — like chlorides from chlorine. Most halides are soluble (dissolve) in water, but <u>silver halides</u> are not (e.g. silver chloride). This fact can be used to test for halide salts because they produce coloured insoluble precipitates, when mixed with silver nitrate solution.

a) What does the term *"precipitate"* mean?

....

....

....

Silver Halide	➔	Precipitate
silver chloride		yellow
silver bromide		white
silver iodide		creamy colour

b) By drawing arrows, <u>*match*</u> the silver halide to the colour of the precipitate formed.

c) Give three uses of chlorine. ....

....

....

....

Q6 What effect will chlorine gas have on damp, blue, litmus paper? ....

....

Q7 In an experiment chlorine was bubbled through sodium bromide solution as shown in the diagram. The clear solution went dark orange/brown.

a) Which is the most reactive, chlorine or bromine?

....

b) *Explain* why the solution went orange/brown.

....

....

....

Chlorine gas

Solution of Sodium bromide

c) What do we call reactions like this where one part of a compound is replaced by another?

....

....

Questions on Salt

Q1 *Rock salt is a mixture of salt and sand and is mined underground. It is possible to obtain a pure sample of salt from rock salt in the laboratory.* Put the following instructions in the *order* they would be carried out in the lab to obtain a *pure* sample of salt.

| a) Filter the solution of rock salt | b) Solid salt is left in the evaporating basin |

| c) Evaporate the water over a Bunsen burner | d) Dissolve the rock salt in water |

e) Warm the water to increase the solubility of the salt

f) Sand is left on the filter paper

g) Place the solution of salt into an evaporating basin

Correct order **1)** .... **2)** .... **3)** .... **4)** .... **5)** .... **6)** .... **7)** ....

Q2 State the main *use* of solid rock salt, that is especially important in the *winter months*.

....

Q3 Name one area of the UK where large *salt deposits* are found. ....

....

Q4 *How* is most of the salt obtained from the ground? ....

....

....

....

....

Q5 What is the *common name* for concentrated sodium chloride solution?

....

Q6 Why is sea water often left in *big open tanks* in some hot countries? ....

....

....

....

Questions on Salt

Q7 Label the diagram below showing the electrolysis of a solution of sodium chloride. Write the appropriate number in the correct white box.

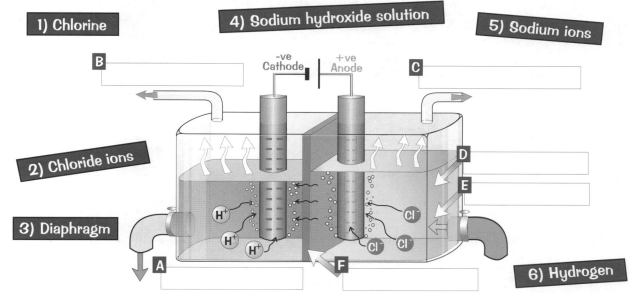

1) Chlorine

4) Sodium hydroxide solution

5) Sodium ions

2) Chloride ions

3) Diaphragm

6) Hydrogen

Q8 *Complete* the following sentences by *filling in* the blanks (words can be used once, more than once or *not at all*).

| industrial   anode   electrolysis   rock salt   brine   cathode |

Sodium chloride has many _____ uses. Salt is mined as

_____. This is purified to give sodium chloride. Useful products

are obtained from a solution of sodium chloride called _____ by passing

electricity through it. This is known as _____. At the _____

chlorine is given off. At the _____ hydrogen is given off. All

the products from the electrolysis of brine can be used, as sodium hydroxide solution is

left in the reaction vessel.

Q9 *Chlorine and hydrogen are formed by the electrolysis of brine.* If a test tube of each were collected, how could you *test* which contained the chlorine and which the hydrogen (other than by looking at their colour)?

....

....

....

....

Questions on the uses of Chlorine

Chlorine is used in bleach which is made by dissolving chlorine in sodium hydroxide solution. Chlorine is used in the production of organic solvents like trichloroethane (which act as degreasers) and is used to manufacture hydrogen chloride. When hydrogen chloride is dissolved in water, a solution of hydrochloric acid is formed. Chlorine is also used to manufacture polyvinyl chloride, which is used for leather-look goods, insulation and rainwear.

Q1   Give *three* uses of chlorine. ....

....

Q2   What is bleach used for? ....

Q3   How are chlorine based compounds useful in swimming pools and in water treatment?

....

Q4   What do you think is meant by the term "organic" solvent? ....

....

Q5   What common everyday use does the degreaser trichloroethane have? *(Clue: non-wet washing)*

....

Q6   *A jet of burning hydrogen is placed into a gas jar full of chlorine to produce hydrogen chloride gas.*

  a) What *colour* is chlorine gas? ....

  b) *The diagram shows the hydrogen chloride gas being dissolved in water to make hydrochloric acid.*

   i)   *Name* the pieces of apparatus A, B and C.

....

....

   ii) How could you show that the solution in C was acidic?

....

   iii) Give a use of hydrochloric acid. ....

....

SECTION SIX — PATTERNS OF BEHAVIOUR

Questions on the uses of Salt Products

Q1 *Electrolysis of brine produces sodium hydroxide, hydrogen and chlorine.*

  a) *Hydrogen is used in the Haber Process.* What is *produced* in the Haber process?

....

  b) *Hydrogen burns to release energy.* What *name* is given to materials that do this?

....

Q2 Hydrogen is used to change oils into fats to make what tasty product?

....

Butter and lard are saturated fats, while sunflower oil and olive oil are unsaturated fats.

Which are better for you, *saturated* or *unsaturated* fats? ....

Q3 Write down *three* uses of sodium hydroxide. ....

....

....

....

Q4 Fill the blanks using the words below.
Words can be used once, more than once or *not at all*.

> sodium   hydrogencarbonate   hydrogen chloride   hydrocarbon
> sodium hydroxide   chlorine   ammonia   hydrogen   fats
> textiles   margarine   oven-cleaners

Brine is electrolysed to give the three products _____ , _____ and

_____ . _____ is used in making PVC, disinfecting drinking

water and in swimming pools. To manufacture PVC it is made into _____

_____ , and this is added to a long chain _____ molecule in

such a way as to form PVC. Hydrogen is used to make _____ such as

_____ . _____ is used to make soaps and detergents,

_____ , paper and _____ such as rayon wool and cotton.

Questions on Acids and Alkalis

Q1 Put a <u>tick</u> in the box next to each of the following statements to indicate which are *true* and which are *false*.

	True	False
All acids are dangerous		
All alkalis are dangerous		
All acids are dissolved in water		
All alkalis are dissolved in water		
Most acids can burn skin		
Alkalis feel soapy		
Acids produce H^+ ions in solution		
Acids taste sweet		
Alkalis produce OH^- ions in solution		
All acids can corrode		
Acids have a pH above 7		
Acids have a pH below 7		
The pH scale goes from 0 to 14		

Q2 Give the *names* of three common bench acids and alkalis, and write out their formulae in the table.

Name of Acid	Formula of Acid		Name of Alkali	Formula of Alkali
(i)			(i)	
(ii)			(ii)	
(iii)			(iii)	

Q3 What do we call a substance with a pH of 7? ....

....

Q4 *Name* a substance that is usually pH 7. ....

....

Questions on Acids and Alkalis

Q5   State which of the following is an *acid* and which is an *alkali*:

a) hydrochloric acid

b) potassium hydroxide

c) sodium hydroxide

d) sulphuric acid

e) nitric acid

Q6   What is an *indicator?* ....

Q7   *Why* are indicators useful? ....

....

Q8   What is a base? *Name* three bases. ....

....

Q9   Draw arrows to match the acid with where it is found or used.

Acid	Found in / used for
Methanoic	Lead acid batteries
Ethanoic	Ant stings
Sulphuric	Pickling onions
Carbonic	Stomach acid
Hydrochloric	Fizzy drinks
Tartaric	Lemons
Citric	Grapes

Q10   Draw arrows from the label to the correct part of the diagram.

Bases

Alkalis

E.g. Magnesium oxide

E.g. Sodium hydroxide

SECTION SIX — PATTERNS OF BEHAVIOUR

Questions on pH and Indicators

Q1 *Colour in* the pH chart with the *correct colours* for Universal Indicator solution.

pH 1   2   3   4   5   6   7   8   9   10 11 12 13 14

←————— ACIDS —————   ————— ALKALIS —————→

NEUTRAL

Q2 What values of pH would you expect for:

a) Citric acid? ....

b) Oven cleaner? ....

c) Sodium chloride (common salt)? ....

d) Sodium hydroxide? ....

e) Lime (calcium hydroxide)? ....

f) Hydrochloric acid? ....

Q3 *Fill in* the blanks with the correct words.

| green | litmus | neutral | red | seven | sodium | citric |
| hydroxide | sulphuric | base | carbonic | purple |

Universal indicator turns a _____ colour in strong acids, _____ in

neutral solutions and _____ in strong alkalis. Another indicator which

changes colour in acid and alkali is _____ .

A solution which is not acid or alkali is said to be _____ , and has a pH of

_____ .

Lemons and oranges contain _____ acid. Fizzy drinks contain _____ acid.

Taking milk of magnesia tablets may help indigestion because they contain a weak

_____ . Oven cleaners contain a strong alkali called _____

_____ . Car batteries contain _____ acid.

Questions on pH and Indicators

Q4   Explain in detail how you could *measure* the pH of a colourless solution.

....

....

....

Q5   Explain in detail how you could *measure* the pH of a brightly coloured solution.

....

....

....

Q6   *The labels have fallen off test tubes with vinegar, water, sulphuric acid, and oven cleaner in. The table below shows the colours observed when pH paper was added to each tube.*

a) Fill in the missing *pH values* in the table.
b) *Identify* which substance is in which tube.

Tube	Colour	pH
1	Red	
2	Orange	
3	Green	
4	Blue	

Tube 1 = ...

Tube 2 = ...

Tube 3 = ...

Tube 4 = ...

Q7   *Complete the table* by adding the correct colour of the indicator in acid or alkali.

Indicator	Colour in solution of:	
	Acid	Alkali
Universal Indicator		
Red Litmus		
Blue Litmus		
Phenolphthalein		

Questions on Acid Reactions - 1

Q1   What is an alkali? ....

Q2   What is a base? ....

Q3   What is a salt? ....

Q4   Which of the following are *acids*, which are *alkalis* and which are *salts?*

   a) hydrochloric acid. ....

   b) sodium chloride. ....

   c) sodium hydroxide. ....

   d) sulphuric acid. ....

   e) nitric acid. ....

   f) calcium nitrate. ....

   g) copper sulphate. ....

Q5   Complete the following *general acid* reactions by filling in the missing products.

A)	Acid + Base → A Salt + _____	
B)	Acid + Metal → A Salt + _____	
C)	Acid + Metal carbonate → A Salt + Water + _____ _____	
D)	Acid + Metal hydrogen-carbonate → A _____ + Water + Carbon dioxide	

Q6   *Link up* the words in the diagram opposite to show the salt produced by each acid.

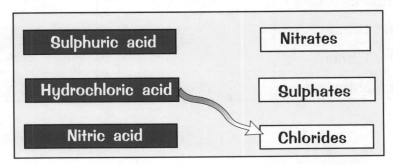

Questions on Acid Reactions - 1

Acid Reaction method.

1) Write out the bits of the equation that you've been given.
2) Work out which general acid reaction you have been given A, B, C or D (see Q.5), and write out the bits of the products you now know — like water or carbon dioxide.
3) Ask yourself *"which acid is reacting"* - this will tell you the salt produced (see Q.6). Then fill in the name of the salt, it's always "metal something", like "copper chloride".

Example question:
What are the products when hydrochloric acid reacts with sodium hydroxide?

1) Write out the bits of the equation that you've been given.

Hydrochloric Acid + Sodium Hydroxide →

2) Work out which general acid reaction you have been given A, B, C or D.

This is type A) Acid + base → salt + water — so fill in the "water" bit.

Hydrochloric Acid + Sodium Hydroxide → _____ + Water

3) Fill in the name of the salt.

Hydrochloric acid is used — so it's a chloride salt that's made.

Hydrochloric Acid + Sodium Hydroxide → Sodium Chloride + Water

Q7 Write out the *products* of the following reactions using the above method.

a) Hydrochloric acid + Potassium hydroxide → _____ + _____

b) Hydrochloric acid + Calcium hydroxide → _____ + _____

c) Hydrochloric acid + Zinc → _____ + _____

Q8 Choose words from the list below to complete the table.

potassium sulphate   potassium nitrate   nitric   sodium hydroxide   sodium sulphate

Acid	Alkali	Salt	Water
Hydrochloric		Sodium chloride	Water
	Magnesium hydroxide	Magnesium nitrate	Water
Sulphuric	Potassium hydroxide		Water

SECTION SIX — PATTERNS OF BEHAVIOUR

120

Questions on Acid Reactions - 2

Q1 *Answer* these questions on neutralisation.

a) What is neutralisation? ....

....

b) Why is neutralisation important to farmers? ....

....

c) What do farmers use to neutralise over-acidic soils? ....

....

Q2 *Two companies are advertising pills which they say relieve stomach ache by neutralising excess stomach acid.*

a) *Describe* what you would do to:

i) check that the pills do in fact neutralise acid? ....

....

ii) discover which pill neutralised the most acid? ....

....

b) *Magnesium Hydroxide is the active ingredient in some indigestion tablets.*

Complete the equation showing how this chemical reacts with hydrochloric acid in the stomach.

Magnesium hydroxide + Hydrochloric acid $\rightarrow$ _____ + _____

Q3 *Read the following passage, which explains how fire extinguishers work.*

Older red fire extinguishers contain sodium hydrogencarbonate solution. When the plunger is pressed down, sulphuric acid mixes and reacts with the sodium hydrogen-carbonate solution, causing a gas to be produced. This makes the pressure build up inside the cylinder, forcing a foam of liquid to be squeezed out of the nozzle.

a) What is the name of the gas produced in the fire extinguisher? ....

b) *Write* a word equation to show the chemical reaction that occurs.

....

Questions on Acid Reactions - 2

Q4 Use the information below to *suggest* the best remedy for the following mishaps:

- Wasp stings are basic.
- Bee stings are acidic.
- Nettles stings are acidic.
- Bicarbonate of soda is alkaline.
- Dock leaves contain alkali.
- Lemon juice is acidic.

a) a wasp sting:— ....

b) a bee sting:— ....

c) nettle sting:— ....

Q5 *Describe* how you might produce a dry sample of the salt *copper sulphate* from copper

oxide and sulphuric acid using normal lab apparatus. ....

....

....

....

....

....

....

Q6 Which acid and which other chemical would you use to make a dry sample of sodium

chloride? ....

....

Q7 Why is it a *bad* idea to use sodium and hydrochloric acid to make sodium chloride?

....

....

....

....

Questions on Metals

Q1   In the circuits below, which bulb, A or B, would light up? _Explain_ your answer in detail.

....

....

....

Q2   _The experiment on the right was set up to show heat transfer along a piece of copper._

   a) Why is wax suitable for holding the drawing pins to

      the copper rod? ....

      ....

   b) What would happen to the drawing pins as the copper wire is heated?

      ....

   c) _Name_ this type of heat transfer. ....

   d) What _term_ is used to describe any material that does not allow heat to flow through it?

      ....

   e) What would you _expect to happen_ if aluminium was tested in the same way? Why?

      ....

      ....

Q3   Look at the table opposite.

   a) Which metal is the most useful for wiring a
      house? _Explain_ your answer _fully_.

      ....

      ....

      ....

Metal	Density (g/cm³)	Electrical Cond. (Relative Units)
Copper	8.9	5.9
Lead	11.3	4.8
Aluminium	2.7	3.8
Iron	7.9	1.0
Zinc	7.1	1.7

   b) Why is aluminium used in overhead power cables instead of lead, even though lead is a

      better conductor? ....

      ....

      ....

Questions on Metals

Q4   *The melting and boiling points of metals are generally high.*

  a)   How does this make them useful? ....

....

  b)   Which metal is the main exception to this? Give one use of this metal.

....

Q5   *Metals are malleable.* What does *malleable* mean and where could this property be useful?

....

....

Q6   Use arrows to *match* up each metal to its use.

1) Copper
2) Lead
3) Aluminium
4) Gold

A) Used for jewellery
B) Used for aircraft
C) Used for wiring
D) Used to keep out radiation

Q7   Complete the table below, showing properties and associated uses for the above four metals. The first one has been done for you.

Metal	Property	Use
Copper	Conducts electricity	Household wiring
Lead		
Aluminium		
Gold		

Q8   *Explain* why gold does not tarnish easily and is found as a native element.

....

....

....

Q9   Draw arrows to match up the substances in the grey boxes with the correct words in the pink boxes.

| Sulphur dioxide | | Basic |

| Sodium oxide | | Acidic |

SECTION SIX — PATTERNS OF BEHAVIOUR

Questions on Non-Metals

Q1 *Look at the Periodic Table below.*

a) *Shade in* the area that represents *non-metals*.

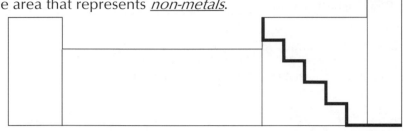

b) Use a *different* colour to shade the group whose elements are in the gas state at room temperature.

Q2 *Look at the table below, then complete parts a) - d).*

Element	Symbol	Melting Point (°C)	Boiling Point (°C)	State at Room Temperature
Sulphur		112	444	
Oxygen		-218	-183	
Bromine		-7	58	
Neon		-248	-246	
Iodine		114	183	

a) Write the symbol of each element in the table.

b) Write in the table the state of each element at a temperature of 20°C.

c) Which non-metal is a liquid at a temperature of 20°C? ....

d) Finish this sentence: "Non-metal usually have a _____ melting point?"

Q3 *Iron is a metal and sulphur is a non-metal. Complete* the table below for both, showing the differences between metals and non-metals. Use the words in the box.

poor conductor	low	good conductor
malleable	high	brittle

Element	Conducts heat	Conducts electricity	Melting Point	Boiling Point	Strength	Density
Iron						
Sulphur						

Q4 *Which of the following properties of non-metals are true and which are false?*

	T	F
Most non-metals are shiny	☐	☐
Most non-metals are brittle and crumbly when solid	☐	☐
Most non-metals are good conductors of heat	☐	☐
Most non-metals are poor conductors of electricity	☐	☐
Most non-metals are gases	☐	☐

SECTION SIX — PATTERNS OF BEHAVIOUR

Questions on Non-Metals

Q5 *Look at the table below of the melting points across one period of the Periodic Table.*

Element	Sodium	Magnesium	Aluminium	Silicon	Phosphorus	Sulphur	Chlorine	Argon
Atomic Number	11	12	13	14	15	16	17	18
Melting Point (°C)	100	620	630	1400	30	110	-100	-190

a) Using the information given, *plot a graph* of the melting points against atomic number using the axes drawn below.

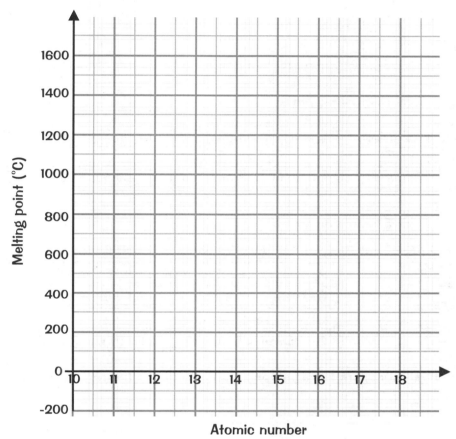

b) Put a circle around the points which represent metals.

c) Compared to the rest of the elements, do the metals have high or low melting points?

....

d) Generally speaking, do non-metals have high or low melting points? ....

e) What is it about silicon's structure that causes it to have a very high melting point.

....

....

Q6 *Non-metal oxides such as Sulphur dioxide are often released into the atmosphere.*
What *substances* would these make when mixed with water? ....

....

Questions on the Reactivity Series

Q1 *The reactivity series is a list of metals.*

a) What do you *understand* by the term "reactivity series"? ....

....

b) Some metals corrode in air. What is meant by *corrosion?* ....

....

c) *Metals react with air, water and acids.* What might you look for in such reactions to

identify which metal is *most reactive?* ....

d) Put these metals in order of reactivity, starting with the most reactive first.

| potassium | gold | aluminium | silver | lead | sodium | iron | copper | zinc |

....

e) Draw arrows to *match* the following metals to the correct statements.

1) Potassium	A) Will not react with water or dilute acid
2) Copper	B) Found alone not combined with anything
3) Iron	C) Very reactive metal
4) Gold	D) Corrodes in air fairly easily forming a substance called rust

Q2 Between which elements are **i)** carbon and **ii)** hydrogen, in the reactivity series?

....

Q3 *Potassium has one electron in its outer shell, which can be easily lost.*

a) Whereabouts in the *reactivity series* would you expect to find potassium? ....

....

b) *Name* one element that could be above potassium in the reactivity series.

....

c) Using the information given below, *place* (by using arrows) metals X and Y in the correct
position in the reactivity series to the right. ☞

| Metal X — | Very reactive, burns in air readily to form a layer of oxide. Reacts violently in water but does not ignite the hydrogen produced. |
| Metal Y — | Corrodes very slowly, needs carbon for extraction from ore. |

Potassium
Magnesium
Iron
Gold
Platinum

Questions on the Reactivity Series

Q4 *Silver, gold and platinum can be found <u>native</u> in the ground as elements and not as compounds. <u>Explain</u> why this can happen.* ....
....
....

Q5 *Aluminium is much more <u>abundant</u> in the Earth's crust than iron, yet it is much <u>more</u> <u>expensive</u> to buy. <u>Explain</u> why it is so expensive, in terms of its reactivity and the cost of extracting it from its ore.* ....
....
....

Q6 Why do you think gold and silver can be worn next to the skin as jewellery, but other metals like sodium cannot? ....
....

Q7 *Metals are shiny. They do however become "dull" with time.*
  a) *<u>Name</u> a metal that would become <u>dull</u> if left in air for only a short time.* ....
  b) *<u>Name</u> a metal that would <u>not</u> become <u>dull</u> easily in air.* ....
  c) *<u>Write</u> the name of a product made from the metal in **a**).* ....

Q8 *<u>Complete</u> the table below.*

Metal	Reaction when heated in air	Compound formed
Calcium		
Zinc		
Iron		
Copper	slow reaction	
Silver		
Potassium		
Gold		
Magnesium		
Platinum	no reaction	
Lead		

SECTION SIX — PATTERNS OF BEHAVIOUR

Questions on Corrosion of Metals

Q1 *Iron is a very cheap and useful metal, but it corrodes easily. The experiment shown here investigates corrosion of iron.*

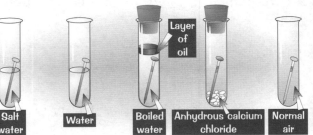

1   2   3   4   5

Salt water   Water   Boiled water   Anhydrous calcium chloride   Normal air

Layer of oil

a) What is the *"common"* name for corroded iron? ....

b) *Write down* in the table below what you would expect to happen in the test tubes shown in the diagram.

Test tube Number	Observations after one week
1	
2	
3	
4	
5	

c) *Explain* the following.

i) The use of anhydrous calcium chloride in tube 4. ....

....

....

ii) The reason the water was boiled in tube 3. ....

....

iii) The reason for using oil in tube 3. ....

....

iv) The use of normal air in tube 5. ....

....

d) What *two things* must be present if iron is to rust? ....

....

Questions on Corrosion of Metals

Q2   *Dee carried out an experiment to see if other metals corroded as quickly as iron.
This is what she set up...*

She put 5cm³ of tap water into each test tube and added 1g of a different metal to each.
She then left them in the lab for a week.

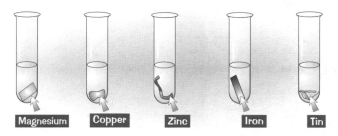

Magnesium   Copper   Zinc   Iron   Tin

a)   Why did she ensure that the metal weighed 1g and measured the 5cm³ of water?

....

....

b)   Which metal(s) would you expect to corrode? *Explain* your answer.

....

....

c)   Which metal(s) would you expect to show no change at all? ....

Q3   *Metals can be treated by galvanising.*

a)   What is *galvanising?* ....

b)   Which *metal* is used to galvanise iron? ....

Q4   Fill in the table using the appropriate words inside the box. Each word may be used once,
more than once or *not at all*.

oiling or greasing the iron	galvanising	painting	coating with aluminium

Item	Best way to prevent rusting
a) Gate	
b) Hull of a ship	
c) Car door	
d) Tools	
e) Machinery	

Questions on Transition Metals

Q1 *The transition metals form a block in the Periodic Table, rather than falling into groups like the other elements.* Colour in the Periodic Table below to show where you would find them.

Q2 Name *four* transition metals you might come across everyday and state what they are used for.

....

....

....

Q3 *The transition metals have properties of typical metals.*
List four properties you would expect a transition element to have.

....

....

....

....

Q4 By drawing arrows *match* the correct colour to each of these compounds.

| 1) Chromium compounds |
| 2) Manganese compounds |
| 3) Copper compound |
| 4) Magnesium compounds |
| 5) Sodium compounds |

| A) White |
| B) Yellow / Orange |
| C) Blue |
| D) Purple |
| E) White |

Q5 *Human blood contains iron and is red.*

a) What *colour* would you expect iron (III) oxide (Fe_2O_3) to be? ....

....

b) Some species of spiders' blood contains copper, what *colour* might their blood be?

....

Questions on Transition Metals

Q6   Answer these questions on the uses of transition metals.

a) Give a _use_ for each of these transition metals: **i)** Iron **ii)** Zinc **iii)** Copper.

....

....

....

b) Why is copper used for household water pipes in _preference_ to iron or zinc?

....

....

Q7   Name _two_ transition elements that could be used to make permanent magnets.

....

Q8   An element, Y, was discovered and found to have properties similar to those of the transition metals.

Fill in the table below for the element Y, giving details of its general properties _(in terms of good, bad, high, low, etc.)._

Conductivity		Density	Malleability	Melting pt
Heat	Electricity			

Q9   Most of the transition elements are used to form alloys in order to improve their physical or chemical properties or to combine their useful properties.

What do you think the following alloys could be _used_ for?

a) Titanium alloy _(light, strong and resistant to corrosion)._ ....

....

b) Iron in the form of stainless steel: 70% iron, 20% chromium, 10% nickel _(hard and does not_

rust). ....

....

c) Bronze: 90% copper, 10% tin _(harder than just pure copper)._ ....

....

Questions on Rates of Reaction

Q1 *Place* these chemical reactions *in order* of speed, starting with the fastest reaction.

| Frying an egg | Striking a match | A car rusting | Concrete setting | Digesting food |

....

....

Q2 *When measuring the rate of a chemical reaction you can consider either the disappearance of a reactant or the production of the product. Look at the apparatus below:*

A   **B**   **C**

For each reaction below, say which of the apparatus, A, B or C above, would be most suitable for measuring its rate.

a) Marble chips with hydrochloric acid	
b) Magnesium and sulphuric acid	
c) Sodium thiosulphate and hydrochloric acid	

Q3 Tick which of the statements below are *true* and which must be *false*.

	True	False		True	False
Catalysts are used up in reactions			Reactions will speed up if they are heated		
Catalysts are specific to certain reactions			Reactions slow down if they are diluted		
Enzymes are biological catalysts			Increasing concentration increases the rate of reaction		
Reactions slow if catalysts are used			Pressure increases the rates of gaseous reactions		
Enzymes increase the activation energy			Reactions are fast at the start		

Q4 *The following changes may or may not speed up the rate of a chemical reaction between an* *acid* *and* *magnesium ribbon*.

Put a tick in the box next to each one that will *speed up* the reaction *(assume that there is initially an excess of acid).*

	A) Heating the acid...
	B) Shaking the flask...
	C) Using more-concentrated acid...
	D) Using powdered metal, not ribbon...
	E) Using twice the volume of acid...
	F) Using a suitable catalyst...
	G) Adding more magnesium...

Questions on Rates of Reaction

Q5   *Products are produced at a rate shown by a rate curve.*

a) On the axes opposite *draw* a *typical rate curve*.

b) Place on the *curve* the following labels concerning the reaction rate:

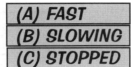

(A) FAST
(B) SLOWING
(C) STOPPED

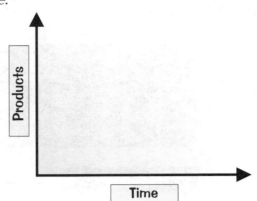

c) Reacting particles must bump into each other with enough energy if a reaction is to occur. Imagine a reaction where two chemicals, ⚪ and ⚪ collide and react. The product would be ⚫⚫ .

The reaction would therefore be: ⚪ + ⚪ ⟶ ⚫⚫

Look at stages A, B and C of the reaction below.

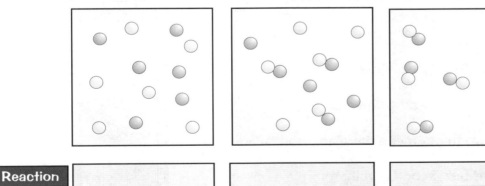

Reaction			

Speed			

Complete the diagrams by placing the following labels below the corresponding pictures.

END	**MIDDLE**	**START**
STOPPED	**FAST**	**SLOWING**

Q6   *Reacting particles do not always collide properly or effectively. Sometimes they miss or collide as described opposite. Complete the diagram to show what might be happening to the particles in each case.*

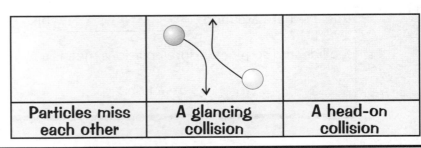

Particles miss each other	A glancing collision	A head-on collision

SECTION SEVEN — REACTION RATES

Questions on The Collision Theory

Use your knowledge of reaction rates to _fill in_ the blanks below. Then put the correct labels on the diagrams.

Word list - may be used more than once
moderate   surface area   faster   collide
particles catalyst   collision theory
concentration   energy   more often
successful   collision

DIAGRAM LABELS
FAST   SLOW   HIGH CONCENTRATION
LOW CONCENTRATION   LARGE
SURFACE AREA   CATALYST PRESENT

Q1

Reactions

Particles can only react if they _____ with enough _____ for

the reaction to take place. This is theory is called the _____ _____.

There are four factors that can change the rate of a chemical reaction, temperature,

_____ , surface area and the use of a suitable _____ .

Q2

Temperature

Increasing the temperature will cause the particles to

move _____ , with more energy.

They will therefore collide _____

_____ and with greater _____ .

These two things mean there are more successful

collisions per second and therefore a

_____ rate of reaction.

FAST	SLOW
HOT	COLD

Q3

Concentration

Increasing the concentration of a reactant simply

means there are more _____ which may

collide and so react. More collisions means a

_____ reaction.

FAST	

Questions on The Collision Theory

Q4

Surface Area

Using powdered reactants instead of a lump means

the _____ _____ is greater, which

means a greater area of reactant is exposed and so

available for a collision. More collisions means a

_____ reaction.

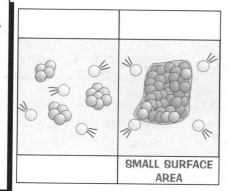

SMALL SURFACE AREA

Q5

Catalysts

Use of a suitable catalyst means that particles

having only _____ energy may react.

This means more _____ collisions are

likely. Some types of catalysts work because one of

the reactants is fixed to a surface. This makes the

chance of a _____ more likely. More

collisions means a _____ reaction.

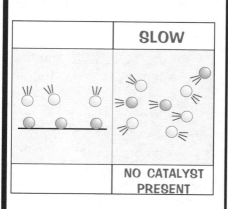

SLOW

NO CATALYST PRESENT

Q6 By drawing arrows, *match* the three descriptions below to these three diagrams.

Particles brush past each other and collide gently

The particles are separated by a barrier and do not collide

The particles collide energetically with each other

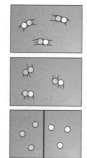

Q7 Circle the sentence that *best describes* the collision theory.

A) Particles collide at random and always react.

B) Collisions between particles often result in a reaction.

C) Reacting particles must collide with enough energy in order to react.

D) Collisions between molecules are sometimes needed before a reaction occurs.

Rates of Reaction Experiments

> The reaction between sodium thiosulphate and hydrochloric acid produces a yellow precipitate of solid sulphur. This makes the solution cloudy and prevents us seeing clearly through it. The cross below the flask in the diagram below will slowly disappear as the sulphur is produced.

Q1   In an experiment to investigate rates of reaction, the time taken for the cross to disappear was recorded. 50cm³ of sodium thiosulphate solution was used and 10cm³ of hydrochloric acid was added. The experiment was repeated at different temperatures.

Temperature (°C)	20	30	40	50	60	70
Time taken (s)	163	87	43	23	11	5

a) Use these results to *plot a graph* on graph paper, with time taken on the vertical axis and temperature on the horizontal axis.

b) *Use the graph* and the collision theory to make a simple conclusion about the effect of temperature on the time taken for the reaction to finish.

....

....

....

....

....

Q2   *When magnesium reacts with acid, hydrogen gas is given off. This can be collected over a period of time as a way of measuring the rate of the reaction.*

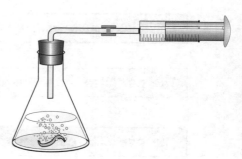

In this experiment 25cm³ of dilute hydrochloric acid was reacted with a small amount of magnesium ribbon (the acid was in excess).

a) Use the results below to *plot a graph* of volume collected (vertical axis) against time (horizontal axis).

Time (s)	0	10	20	30	40	50	60	70	80	90	100
Vol. hydrogen (cm³)	0	9	18	27	36	44	50	54	56	57	57

Rates of Reaction Experiments

Q2 cont...

b) *Mark* on your graph where the reaction is at a constant rate.

c) *What volume* of hydrogen was collected in the first 25 seconds? ....

d) *How long* did it take to collect 40cm³ of hydrogen? ....

e) *Sketch* on the *same graphs* the lines you would expect if the experiment was repeated using 25cm³ of:

   more concentrated acid .... mark this line A

   less concentrated acid .... mark this line B

Q3 *A similar experiment was carried out to investigate how changing the temperature can effect the rate of reaction between acid and magnesium. The graph below shows results from such an experiment. The acid is increasingly warmer in experiments 1, 2 and 3 .*

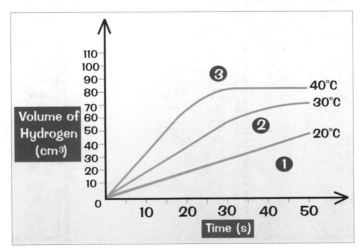

a) Which temperature produces the quickest reaction? ....

b) *Another way of finding out which reaction is quickest is to work out the "rate". The rate is how much product is made divided by the time taken to make it.*

   i) What volume of hydrogen is produced in the first 20 seconds of each experiment?

   ....

   ....

   ii) Divide each answer by 20 to get the rates (in cm³/s) for each case. ....

   ....

   ....

   iii) Generally which conditions of temperature produce the fastest rates? ....

More Questions on Rates of Reaction

Q1 *Marble chips react with acid to produce carbon dioxide gas. This loss of gas allows the reaction to be followed by recording the mass every 30 seconds on a balance.*

The experiment was repeated with the same concentration and temperature of acid and the same total mass of marble, but using different sized pieces.

> Experiment 1 .... large marble chips and acid.
>
> Experiment 2 .... small marble chips and acid.
>
> Experiment 3 .... powdered marble chips and acid.

a) In carrying out this experiment, *what factors* are kept constant? ....

....

b) Use the results in the tables to *work out* the total mass lost after every 30 seconds.

Experiment 1

E.g. 100-99.8

Time (s)	Mass (g)	Mass Lost (g)
0	100	0
30	99.8	
60	99.6	
90	99.4	
120	99.2	
150	99.0	
180	98.8	
210	98.6	
240	98.45	
270	98.30	
300	98.20	
330	98.15	
360	98.15	

Experiment 2

Time (s)	Mass (g)	Mass Lost (g)
0	100	0
30	99.7	
60	99.4	
90	99.1	
120	98.8	
150	98.6	
180	98.4	
210	98.3	
240	98.2	
270	98.15	
300	98.15	
330	98.15	
360	98.15	

Experiment 3

Time (s)	Mass (g)	Mass Lost (g)
0	100	0
30	99.0	
60	98.5	
90	98.3	
120	98.2	
150	98.15	
180	98.15	
210	98.15	
240	98.15	
270	98.15	
300	98.15	
330	98.15	
360	98.15	

c) *Plot* the mass lost against time for each experiment on the same set of axes.

d) Which experiment was the *fastest?* ....

e) *Explain* your answer to part **d)** in terms of particles and collisions. ....

....

....

f) Why do all the graphs finish at the *same point?* ....

....

g) Why does the gradient — and hence the rate — *DECREASE* as the experiment goes on?

....

....

More Questions on Rates of Reaction

Q2 The decomposition (breakdown) of hydrogen peroxide (H_2O_2) to water and oxygen is very slow. However, it may be speeded up by using a suitable catalyst.

Time (s)	Volume of oxygen collected (cm^3)		
	Manganese oxide	Copper oxide	Iron (III) oxide
0	0	0	0
10	15	3	1
20	30	6	2
30	45	9	3
40	60	12	4
50	70	15	5
60	78	18	6
70	85	21	7
80	90	24	8
90	92	27	9
100	92	30	10

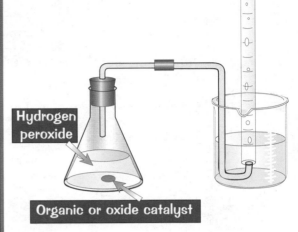

Hydrogen peroxide

Organic or oxide catalyst

a) Use these results to *plot three curves* on the same graph so that you can compare them easily.

b) Which *oxide* is the best catalyst for this reaction? ....

c) Give a *reason* for your answer. ....

d) What is a *catalyst?* ....

e) *Explain briefly* how catalysts are thought to speed up reactions. ....

....

....

Q3 The breakdown of hydrogen peroxide may also be catalysed by enzymes in living cells, particularly those in liver and potato. Study the graphs right, which show typical results from such an experiment.

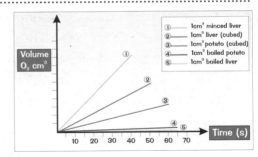

a) Out of potato and liver, which contains the most *effective* enzymes? ....

b) What is the effect of *boiling the living tissue?* ....

c) Why is the rate *faster* with minced liver than the cubed liver? ....

....

d) *Enzymes are biological catalysts.* State *two* facts you know about enzymes.

....

SECTION SEVEN — REACTION RATES

Questions on Catalysts

Q1 *The diagrams to the right show how 0.5g of zinc and 0.5g of copper react with dilute sulphuric acid.*

a) Does the *copper metal* react with dilute sulphuric acid?

....

b) Does *zinc* react with dilute sulphuric acid?

....

c) How do *zinc and copper* together react with dilute sulphuric acid?

....

d) *Describe* what copper does to the rate of reaction in tube 3. ....

....

....

> **Tube 3 was left for several hours until the reaction was finished. The copper was removed, dried and weighed. Its mass was 0.5g.**

e) What does this tell you about the *action* of copper in speeding up the reaction between

zinc and dilute sulphuric acid? ....

....

....

Q2 *Catalytic converters are found in almost every new car. Their function is to clean up exhaust emissions and reduce pollution.*

a) Name *three* polluting gases found in "normal" car exhaust fumes.

....

b) What *"harmless gases"* are they converted into? ....

c) Why do all cars with a catalytic converter use *unleaded petrol*? ....

....

....

d) *Some people have argued that catalytic converters do more harm than good. Suggest one*

possible argument they might use. ....

....

Questions on Catalysts

Q3 *Trypsin is an enzyme that catalyses the breakdown of protein. Photographic film has a protein layer that holds the silver compounds in place (these appear black). The ability of trypsin to break down protein depends on temperature. The experiment below investigates this. Strips of photographic film were each left for ten minutes in test tubes at the temperatures shown.*

Temperature: 20°C   25°C   30°C   35°C   40°C

a) From these results, what appears to be the *optimum temperature?*

....

b) Explain what happens to the enzyme at temperatures *above* the optimum temperature.

....

....

c) *Why* does trypsin have the particular optimum temperature as demonstrated in this

experiment? ....

....

Q4 *The browning of apples after being cut is an enzyme-catalysed reaction (enzymes speed up this reaction). An apple was cut into slices and placed in different conditions.*

1 2 3 4

In lab | Fridge | With lemon | Dipped in boiling water

75% browning | 40% browning | Slightly less than 10% browning | Slightly less than 10% browning

a) What *conclusion* about the conditions which these enzymes "prefer" can be made by

comparing results 1 and 2? ....

....

b) What *conclusion* about the conditions which these enzymes "prefer" can be made from

results 1 and 3? ....

....

c) What does *result 4* tell you about the nature of these catalysts? ....

....

Questions on Enzymes

Q1 Unfortunately the head teacher spilled custard down his clean white shirt. A group of year 10 students offered to find the best way to get it clean. They cut up the shirt into squares (as you do), and tested each with a different wash to find the best way to remove the stain.

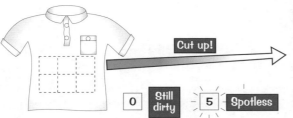

Treatment	How clean?
A) Hand wash in cold water	0
B) Warm wash with ordinary powder	3
C) 70°C wash with "Ace bio powder"	3
D) 40°C wash with "Ace bio powder"	5
E) Cold wash with "Ace bio powder"	3

a) Which wash gave the *best result?* ....

b) What is the special ingredient in *"bio"* or *"biological"* powders? ....

c) For what reason did tests C and E give poor result? ....

....

....

Q2 *Cheese goes mouldy after a while.*

a) What causes cheese and other foods to go off? ....

b) Why does keeping cheese in the fridge help to keep it fresh for longer? ....

....

c) *Explain* why meat or vegetables in the freezer stay fresh for months. ....

....

d) Why must you use defrosted foods quickly? ....

....

....

Q3 *Loads of cream cakes were put in different places in the kitchen.*

In which order should the cakes be eaten if each is to be enjoyed as *FRESH* as possible?

....

....

....

....

Questions on Enzymes

Q4 *The enzymes in yeast help to produce energy from sugar by breaking down glucose into carbon dioxide and ethanol.*

The experiment was repeated at different temperatures and the volume of carbon dioxide gas recorded every 30 minutes. The results are shown in the table below.

a) Use the results to *plot eight graphs* on graph paper — use the same set of axes. For each graph label the axes as below.

(For easy comparison, use different colours for each temperature).

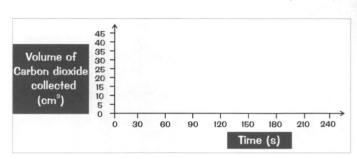

Time (s)	Volume of Carbon dioxide collected (cm³) at temperature (°C)							
	20	25	30	35	40	45	50	55
0	0	0	0	0	0	0	0	0
30	0	0	1	3	3	1	1	0
60	0	0	2	6	6	2	2	0
90	0	1	3	9	9	3	3	0
120	1	1	5	13	13	4	3	0
150	1	2	7	18	18	6	4	0
180	2	3	10	25	25	8	5	0
210	3	5	14	35	35	10	6	0
240	4	7	18	45	45	12	7	0

b) From your graphs, which temperature(s) appear to be the best *working temperature(s)* for this enzyme? ....

c) Use this graph to suggest an *optimum temperature* range for this reaction. ....

d) *Explain* what happens to the enzyme at temperatures *above* this optimum temperature.

....

....

e) *The process of fermentation is very important. Name two* major products that depend on

fermentation. ....

....

Q5 *Bacteria are used in the food industry as well as yeast.*

a) Milk is the starting material for which *two* major foods

made using bacteria? ....

....

b) Why is *pasteurised milk* normally used instead of fresh milk? ....

....

....

Questions on Reversible Reactions

Q1 *Look at the two diagrams below. In diagram A hydrochloric acid and ammonia are reacting to make ammonium chloride.* 👉

Conc. Hydrochloric acid on cotton wool

Conc. Ammonia on cotton wool

A Ammonium chloride

B

Red litmus paper going blue - showing ammonia to be present

Ammonium chloride

Heat

In the diagram B, ammonium chloride is turning into ammonia. ☞

a) Write *equations* to represent the reactions taking place in diagrams A and B.

A) ....

B) ....

b) The reaction in diagram B requires heat to be absorbed. Will the reaction taking place in diagram A absorb or give out heat? ....

c) Explain your answer to **b)** in terms of reversible reactions. ....

....

....

Q2 *Copper sulphate can be either a blue or white crystalline powder.*

Blue Powder ⟶ White Powder

a) How can you change the *blue powder* to a *white powder?* ....

....

b) How can you *reverse* the process and turn white powder to blue? ....

....

Q3 Complete these sentences by filling in the blanks with the words provided.

| *products* | *reversible* | *point* | *reverse* |

_____ reactions are chemical reactions where the _____

can be converted back into the reactants under suitable conditions. Some reactions

reach a _____ where the forward and the _____ reaction

are happening at the same rate. The reaction is then in equilibrium.

SECTION SEVEN — REACTION RATES

Questions on Energy Transfer

Q1 _Fill in the blanks_ in the following passage (the words can be used more than once).

energy	exothermic	endothermic	cold	taken in
hot	given out	negative	energy	break	made

A reaction that gives out _____ is called an _____ reaction.

A reaction that takes in _____ is called an _____ reaction.

_____ reactions can feel _____ as energy is _____ _____ .

_____ reactions can feel _____ as energy is _____ _____ .

For _____ reactions the energy change is positive as heat is needed, e.g. +250kJ. A _____ energy change indicates an exothermic reaction as heat is released. E.g. -250kJ.

Virtually all chemical reactions involve _____ changes. Whether they are _____ or _____ depends on the balance between the _____ needed to _____ bonds in the reactants, and the _____ released when bonds are _____ in the products.

Q2 Classify these reactions or changes as _exothermic_ or _endothermic_.

a) Burning a fuel. ....

b) Condensing a vapour. ....

c) Evaporation. ....

d) Neutralising an acid. ....

e) Thermal decomposition of copper carbonate. ....

f) Rapid oxidation of iron. ....

g) Rapid dissolving of ammonium nitrate. ....

h) .... **i)** ....

Brrrr....!

Phew!

The Killer Kool-Pak
och!
For all your sporting injuries..

THE ROASTY
HAND WARMER

SECTION SEVEN — REACTION RATES

SCG TRIAL EXAM

General Certificate of Secondary Education

Science: Double Award
(Coordinated and Modular)
Foundation Paper: Trial Examination

Monday 7 June 1999 9.30am — 11.00 am

Centre name									
Centre number					Candidate number				
Surname									
Other names									

(F)

In addition to this paper you will need a:
- Pen
- Pencil
- Calculator
- Ruler

Time
- 1 hour 30 minutes.

Instructions to candidates
- Write your name and other details in the spaces provided above.
- Answer **all** the questions in this paper.
- Write your answers in this combined question paper/answer book.
- Write your answers in blue or black ink or ballpoint pen.
- Do all rough work on the paper.

Information for candidates
- The number of marks is given in brackets at the end of each question or part-question.
- Marks will not be deducted for incorrect answers.
- You are reminded of the need for good English and clear presentation.
- In calculations show clearly how you work out your answers.

For examiner's use	
Page 147	
148	
149	
150	
151	
152	
153	
154	
155	
156	
Total	

1) The diagram shows the arrangement of particles in iron, water and air.

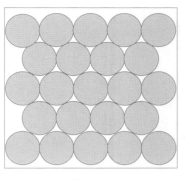
Iron

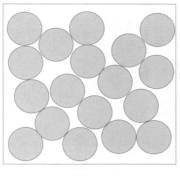
Water

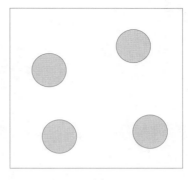
Air

a) How can you tell that air is a gas?

....

....

....

(1 mark)

b) Air can be put into a bike tyre by using a hand pump.

Plunger

Explain using the diagrams at the top of the page why air can be easily squashed by the plunger.

....

....

....

(1 mark)

c) If the pump was filled with water (a liquid) and a finger placed over the end, why would it be difficult to squash?

....

....

(2 marks)

SECTION EIGHT — SCG TRIAL EXAM

2) The structure of an atom of an element is shown below.

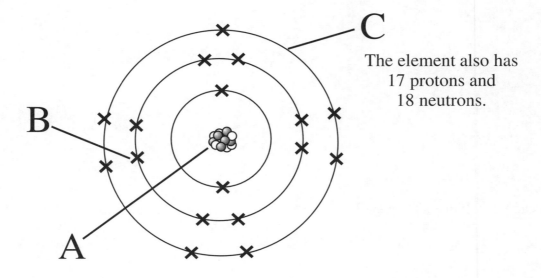

The element also has
17 protons and
18 neutrons.

Using the information in the picture above and your periodic table answer the following.
a) i) In which group of the Periodic Table would you find this element?

....
(1 mark)

ii) In which period of the Periodic Table would you find this element?

....
(1 mark)

iii) What is the mass number of this element?

....
(1 mark)

iv) What is the atomic number of this element?

....
(1 mark)

b) i) What do labels A, B and C represent?

A represents ....

B represents ....

C represents ....
(3 marks)

ii) What particles are found in A?

....
(1 mark)

iii) What is the symbol for this element?

....
(1 mark)

3) Element Z has the following properties:

- It has a melting point of 708°C.
- It conducts electricity well.
- It conducts heat well.
- It reacts quickly with water.
- It forms giant structures with non-metals.

a) Is Z a metal or a non-metal?

....
(1 mark)

b) Is Z a solid, liquid or gas at room temperature and pressure?

....
(1 mark)

c) Which group is Z probably in?

....
(1 mark)

d) Would the oxide of Z have a high or low melting point?

....
(1 mark)

4) The metals shown below were put in hydrochloric acid. The diagram shows what happened.

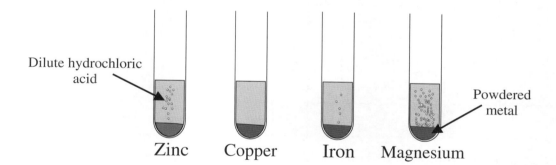

Dilute hydrochloric
acid

Powdered
metal

Zinc   Copper   Iron   Magnesium

Look at the diagram and place the metals in the order of their reactivity, with the most reactive at the top and the least reactive at the bottom.

Most reactive

....

....

....

....

Least reactive

(1 mark)

SECTION EIGHT — SCG EXAM

5) 10g of marble chips were placed into 100cm³ of hydrochloric acid at 25ºC.
The gas produced was collected in a gas syringe over a period of time. The results are shown below.

Gas Syringe

Conical Flask

Hydrochloric acid

Marble chips

Time/s	Volume of gas collected/cm³
30	10
60	20
90	29
120	41
150	45
180	47
210	47
240	47

a) Draw a graph of the volume of carbon dioxide gas produced against time.   *(4 marks)*

b) From the graph, at what time is the reaction the fastest: 90 seconds or 150 seconds?

....
                                                                                                                    (1 mark)

c) Explain how you worked out your answer to b).

....

....
                                                                                                                    (1 mark)

d) The reaction was repeated and was found to be faster when more concentrated acid was used.
Explain, in as much detail as possible, why the reaction was quicker.

....

....

....
                                                                                                                    (3 marks)

SECTION EIGHT — SCG EXAM

6) Find caesium ($^{133}_{55}$Cs) on your periodic table (at the front of the book).

The melting points of some alkali metals are shown below.

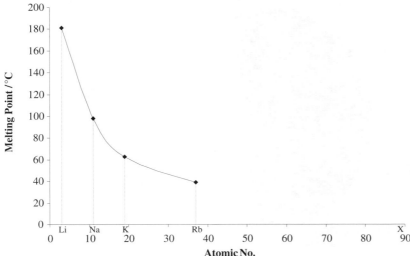

a) Caesium is an alkali metal. What group is caesium in? ....

(2 marks)

b) In theory what simple test could you do to show that caesium is a metal?

....

(1mark)

c) Why might this be difficult or dangerous in practice?

....

(1mark)

d) From the graph estimate the melting point of caesium.

....

(2 marks)

e) Predict the following about caesium:

   i) How caesium reacts with water.

      ....

      ....

      ....

(3 marks)

   ii) Whether the solution made in i) will be acidic or alkaline.

      ....

(1 mark)

f) Caesium forms a compound with chlorine. Describe how caesium can chemically bond to chlorine.

....

....

....

(2 marks)

7) The pie chart below shows some uses of aluminium.

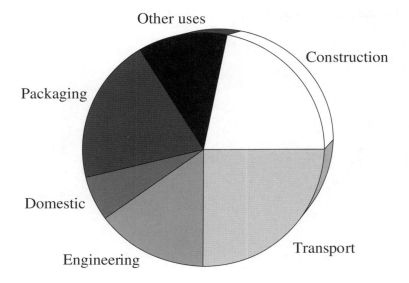

a) Give four uses of aluminium and state in which section of the pie chart they would be included.

....

....

....

....

(4 marks)

b) Aluminium is a useful metal, but it often needs to be strengthened by alloying.

i) What is an alloy?

....

(1 mark)

ii) A particle-slip diagram can be used to explain how aluminium is strengthened by alloying. Draw in the box below how the atoms of aluminium and magnesium might be arranged in an alloy of 90% aluminium and 10% magnesium.

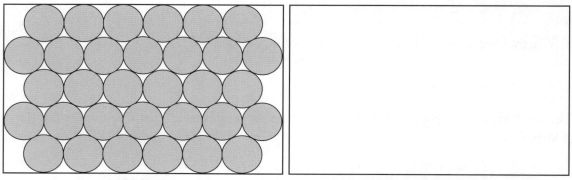

Aluminium   Aluminium/magnesium alloy

(2 marks)

iii) The bar chart gives information about three metals.

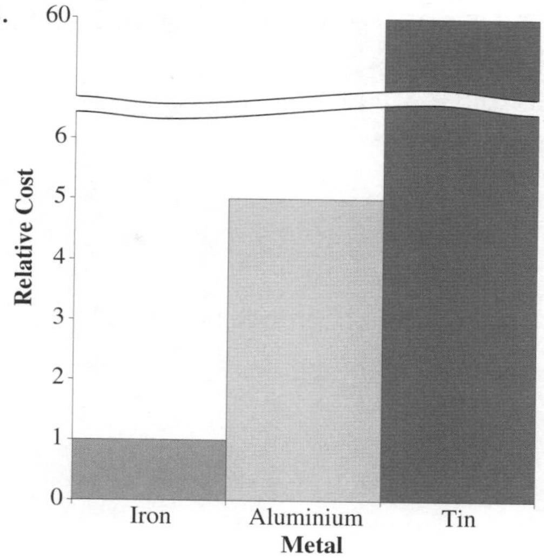

Why is it important to recycle aluminium?

....

....

....

(1 mark)

iv) Tin is used to coat steel (iron) drinks cans. Why is this not necessary for aluminium?

....

(1 mark)

v) Despite the relatively low cost of iron, steel cans are recycled. Give two reasons for this.

....

....

(2 marks)

c) Industrially, aluminium is extracted from its ore by electrolysis in an electrolytic reduction cell, as shown below.

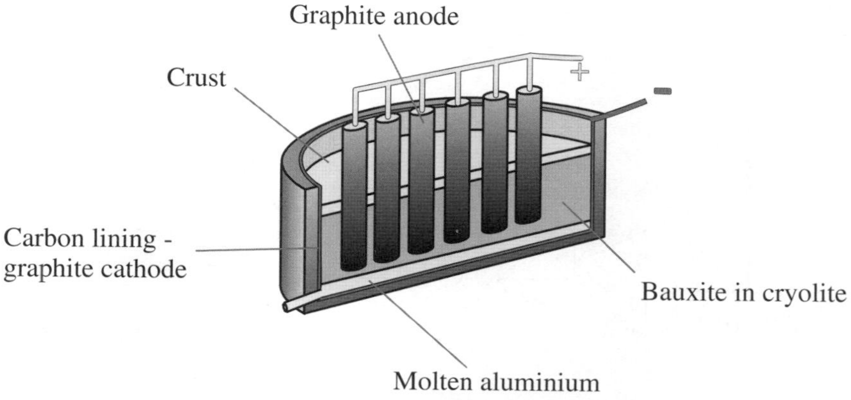

i) Give the chemical name for the main aluminium compound in bauxite.

....

(1 mark)

ii) Why is the bauxite melted?

....

(1 mark)

iii) Why is the apparatus known as a reduction cell?

....

(1 mark)

iv) What is produced at the cathode?

....

(1 mark)

SECTION EIGHT — SCG EXAM

Leave
margi
blank

8) The diagram shows a section through the Earth.

a) Label X and Y.

X= .... Y= ....
(2 marks)

b) Give one difference between layers X and Y.

....

....

....

....
(1 mark)

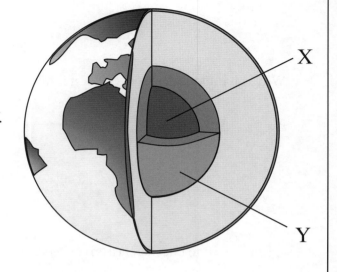

Look at this diagram showing the rock cycle.

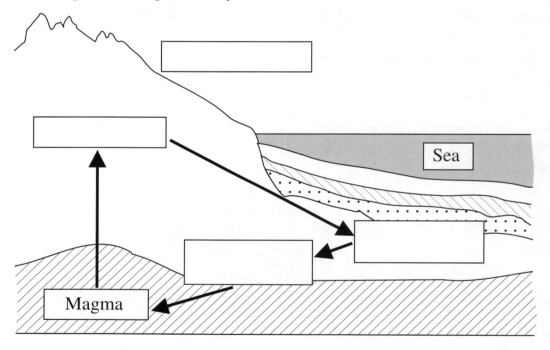

c) Place the following labels on the diagram.

| weathering | | sedimentary rocks |

| metamorphic rocks | | igneous rocks |

(4 marks)

d) Weathering involves the breaking down of rocks into smaller rock fragments. Weathering may come about as a result of the action of such things as ice, acidic rainwater, or plant roots. Explain in as much detail as possible how each of these can bring about weathering.

i) Water freezing.

....

....

....

....

....

....

(3 marks)

ii) Acidic rain.

....

....

....

....

....

....

(3 marks)

iii) Plant roots.

....

....

....

....

....

....

(3 marks)

9) Methane (natural gas) is used for heating and cooking in the home. When it burns it releases heat energy.

a) Give an alternative name for burning.

....
(1 mark)

b) What is the name given to a reaction in which energy is given out?

....
(1 mark)

c) Where in or around Britain might you find deposits of methane?

....
(1 mark)

d) Methane is a hydrocarbon. What is a hydrocarbon?

....
(1 mark)

e) Heat is produced when hydrocarbons burn completely. Name two chemical substances that are produced in this process.

....
(2 marks)

f) Incomplete combustion is when a chemical does not burn properly due to a limited supply of oxygen.

i) What dangerous gas might be produced during the incomplete combustion of a hydrocarbon such as methane?

....
(1 mark)

ii) Why is this gas particularly dangerous?

....
(1 mark)

SECTION EIGHT — SCG EXAM